# Gollancz Children's Encyclopaedia of Birds

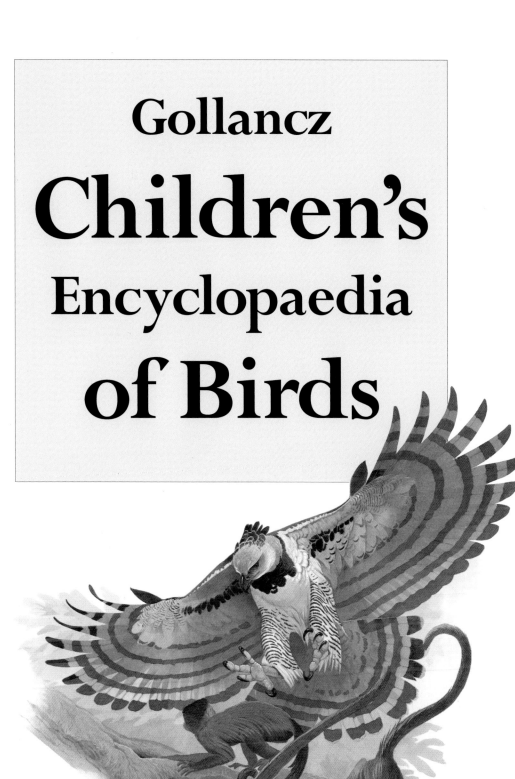

Blue and yellow macaw and palm cockatoo

Previous page: Harpy eagle

Facing page: Toco toucan

# Gollancz
# Children's
# Encyclopaedia
# of Birds

**JINNY JOHNSON**

Victor Gollancz
LONDON

**A Marshall Edition**
This book was conceived, edited and designed by
Marshall Editions
170 Piccadilly, London W1V 9DD

First published in Great Britain 1996
by Victor Gollancz
An imprint of the Cassell Group
Wellington House, 125 Strand, London WC2R 0BB

A catalogue record for this book is available from the British Library

ISBN 0 575 06278 9

The right of Jinny Johnson to be identified as author of this work has
been asserted by her in accordance with the Copyright, Designs and
Patents Act, 1988

Consultant:  Dr Malcolm Ogilvie
Managing editor:  Kate Phelps
Art editor:  Dave Goodman
Picture editor:  Zilda Tandy
Copy editor:  Isabella Raeburn

Editorial director:  Cynthia O'Brien
Art director:  Branka Surla
Production:  Janice Storr

Printed and bound in Italy

# Contents

Common tern

Pochard and ducklings

Great skua

# Foreword

Birds are among the most successful of all the world's animals, and have conquered air, land and water. While a few species, such as penguins, manage very well without the power of flight, others, such as swifts and frigatebirds, may be on the wing for months at a time, landing only to nest. Birds are found on all continents, including the icy land of Antarctica, and on the remotest islands. They are found at heights of more than 8,000 metres in the Himalayas and around the shores of the Dead Sea at 400 metres below sea level. They live in both oceans and inland waters, from tiny ponds to great lakes. Birds such as loons and auks can dive to depths of 60 metres and stay submerged for as long as three minutes.

Humans have been intrigued by birds for thousands of years. Although they have been hunted for food and sport, birds have also been the inspiration for paintings, poetry and music. Nowadays, more and more people enjoy watching birds, observing their wonderful powers of flight and their infinite variety of plumages. For many of us, our first experience of wildlife is seeing birds feeding in gardens and parks or nesting on houses or other buildings.

It is generally accepted that there are just over 9,000 different species of birds in the world. (The number is not exact, because it is not always certain whether two or more

**King penguin**

similar birds are separate species or different forms of the same species.) A few new species are described each year, but, sadly, some are also disappearing. Nearly 100 species have become extinct – disappeared completely – in the last 400 years and, largely because of the activities of humans, that rate is increasing. The destruction of habitats, such as the clearing of rainforests and the draining of marshes, is an obvious cause of problems, but most extinctions have occurred after the introduction of animals and plants from other places to remote islands. The birds that live naturally on these islands have been unable to cope with new predators or competitors.

The situation remains gloomy, with more than 150 species throughout the world thought to be in danger of extinction. Now that the reasons for past extinctions are better understood, however, there is hope that enough can be done to save these superb creatures for future generations to enjoy.

DR MALCOLM OGILVIE

# What is a bird?

There are more than 9,000 different species of bird. The vast majority can fly and their structure reflects this. A typical bird has a strong but light body, two legs and a pair of wings. The wings are, in fact, modified forelimbs. All birds are covered with feathers – and are the only creatures to have them. Feathers are made of keratin, a protein that also makes up the scales on reptiles and the hair and nails of humans and other mammals.

Feathers keep a bird warm and streamline its body. They are windproof and sometimes waterproof. For many birds the colour of their feathers helps them attract mates or hide from enemies. It is the large, strong feathers on the wings and tail that enable birds to fly.

All birds have a beak with which they can pick up food, break open nuts and hard seeds and tear apart flesh. Beaks vary widely in shape depending on diet. Birds of prey have large hooked beaks, for example, while the beaks of insect eaters are fine and slender.

## A bird's egg

A young bird grows inside an egg. The yolk is its food supply and the surrounding layers of egg white, called albumen, protect it from sudden movements or changes in temperature. The hard shell encloses and protects the whole structure. The shells of small eggs may be only the thickness of a page of this book, but the shell of an ostrich egg can be more than 2 centimetres thick.

Growth region

Yolk

Egg white (albu

Shell

Embryo
(baby bird)

Yolk

All birds lay eggs. It would be impossible for birds to carry their growing young inside their bodies as mammals do because they would become too heavy to fly. The embryo is protected inside a hard-shelled egg, which is usually kept warm by the parents, normally in a nest. The incubation period – the time taken for the fertilized egg to grow into a chick and break out of the shell – varies from about 10 to 12 days in small birds, such as warblers and wrens, to as many as 84 days in albatrosses.

Some young birds hatch in a poorly developed state and are completely dependent on their parents to keep them safe and bring them food. Even when they are able to leave the nest, the young birds may remain with their parents for weeks or even months. Other young are able to move around and find food for themselves almost immediately after birth.

Not all birds fit exactly into these two groups, however. Hawks, for example, hatch covered with downy feathers. But, although they are able

## A blackbird chick

24 hours

Three days

One week

Two weeks

## A typical bird and wing

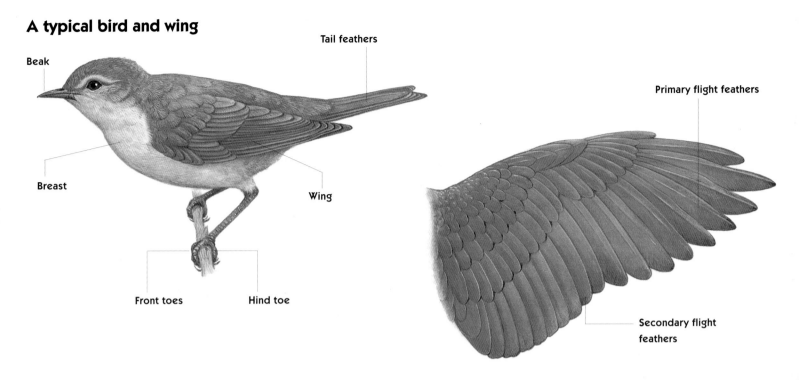

Beak

Tail feathers

Primary flight feathers

Breast

Wing

Secondary flight feathers

Front toes

Hind toe

Gannets demonstrate their skill in the air as they swoop down to the rocks where they lay their eggs and rear their young.

to move around, they stay in the nest and are fed and cared for by their parents for several weeks.

Birds are among the best loved of all animals, perhaps because they are all around us and easy to see in our everyday lives, even in the cities. If you would like to see more birds, try putting a feeder on a window ledge or in your garden in the winter months, when food is harder for birds to come by. Watch and you will be surprised by the number of different kinds of birds that pay a visit.

The young of songbirds and some other types of bird, such as pigeons, swifts and woodpeckers, are born naked, blind and helpless. They are dependent on the care of their parents until they are fully feathered and able to fly. At the other extreme are the young of birds such as ducks, geese and waders. They hatch covered with warm downy feathers and their eyes open. They move around and find food for themselves only hours after hatching.

## A duckling

24 hours

One to two weeks

Four to five weeks

**9**

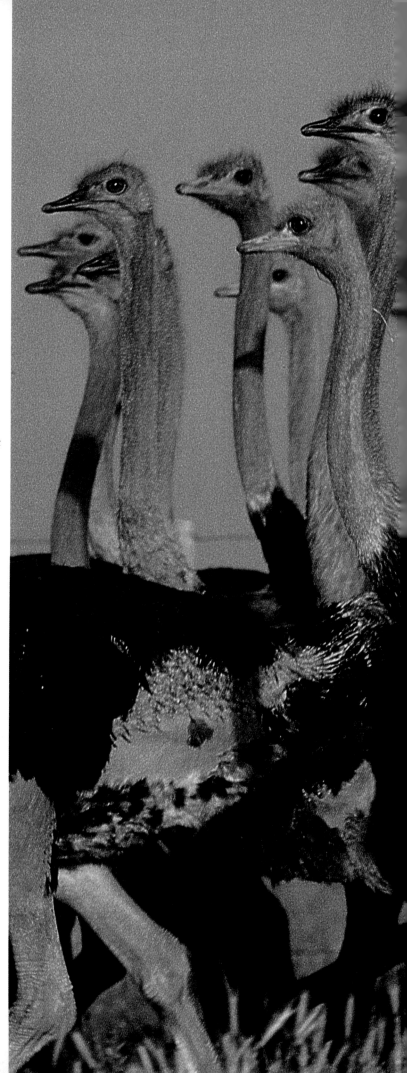

# Ground birds and game birds

---

*Glittering peacocks and speedy ostriches
are among the many birds that live at
ground level instead of soaring in the air.*

---

Not all birds are high fliers. Many spend most of their
life on the ground, where they scratch around to find
food. Some of the most interesting ground-living birds are
ratites, or running birds. They include species such as the
ostrich and emu, as well as rheas, cassowaries and kiwis.
None of these birds can fly – they do have wings but
these are too small to be used for flight. Instead, the
ratites rely on fast running to escape from danger, and
all but the kiwi have long, powerful legs. The ostrich is
both the largest and the fastest running of all birds.

Game birds, too, spend most of their time on the
ground, but they can fly and often roost in trees at night.
This large and varied group includes more than 260
different species – birds such as pheasants, grouse,
guineafowl and malleefowl. Most have well-rounded
bodies and short, strong legs – the domestic fowl is a
typical example. They are known as "game birds" because
certain species, such as grouse and pheasants, have long
been hunted and shot in some parts of the world.

Also included in this chapter are ground-living birds
from other families, such as the great bustard, satin
bowerbird, Pallas's sandgrouse and greater roadrunner.
All of these birds can fly but spend most of their lives at
ground level.

---

*Long-legged ostriches cannot fly but can run
at speeds of more than 65 kilometres an hour
and easily outrun most of their enemies.*

---

# How ground birds and game birds live

Ground-living birds are not fierce hunters. They lead peaceful lives, feeding mostly on seeds, leaves and shoots, which they find on the ground. Some also eat insects and even small reptiles. The long-legged, flightless birds, such as ostriches, rheas and emus, live in dry grasslands and semi-desert and often have to travel far to find food. As they stand head down to eat, they are vulnerable to attack by enemies and must raise their heads from time to time to keep watch for any danger.

Ostriches and rheas lay their eggs in shallow nests scraped in the ground. Emus make a low platform of twigs and branches. Male and female ostriches share the care of the eggs, but male emus and rheas do all of the incubation. The male emu eats extra amounts of food before the breeding season to build up his reserves of body fat because he hardly eats at all while incubating the eggs.

Pheasants and other game birds scratch around for seeds and berries with their stout legs and strong claws. Some, such as the bobwhite quail, also take the seeds of crops such as maize and soya. Game birds usually make simple nests on the ground. Their chicks hatch with a full covering of soft feathers, called down, and leave the nest soon after hatching.

**Male emu guarding his clutch of eggs from enemies. Once the chicks hatch, he continues to take care of them for up to 18 months.**

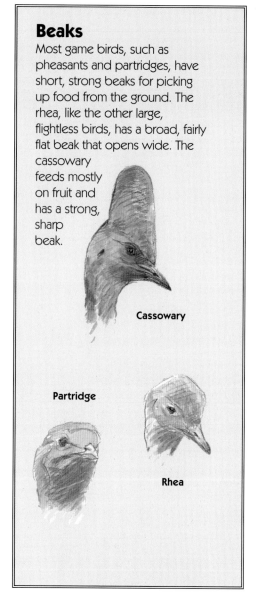

## Beaks

Most game birds, such as pheasants and partridges, have short, strong beaks for picking up food from the ground. The rhea, like the other large, flightless birds, has a broad, fairly flat beak that opens wide. The cassowary feeds mostly on fruit and has a strong, sharp beak.

**Cassowary**

**Partridge**

**Rhea**

**Bobwhite quail eating the seeds of farm crops.**

**Golden pheasant scratching in the ground for food.**

**Malleefowl** testing the temperature of its mound-shaped nest, which is made of rotting plants and sandy soil.

**Kiwi** using its long beak to find food among dead leaves on the forest floor.

### Feet

Like most birds, pheasants and other game birds have four toes, three facing forwards and one backwards. The ostrich has large, strong feet, each with only two toes. If in danger, the ostrich can kick powerfully, slashing an enemy with the sharp claw on its large toe.

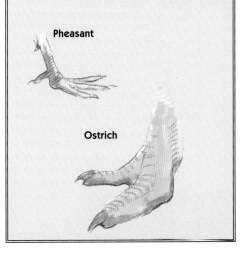

**Pheasant**

**Ostrich**

**Ostrich,** with its head down, feeding on seeds and leaves, which it finds on the ground.

| MAIN FAMILIES OF GROUND BIRDS AND GAME BIRDS |
|---|
| **Ostrich.** 1 species. Large, flightless, fast-running bird. |
| **Rheas.** 2 species. Large, flightless birds. |
| **Emu.** 1 species. Large, flightless bird with shaggy feathers. |
| **Cassowaries.** 3 species. Large, flightless birds with bony casques on their heads. |
| **Kiwis.** 3 species. Small, flightless birds with long beaks. |
| **Tinamous.** 46 species. Plump, ground-living birds. |
| **Megapodes.** 19 species. Ground birds which lay their eggs in mounds of plants and sandy soil. |
| **Guans and curassows.** 45 species. Large, forest-living birds with long, broad tails. |
| **Turkeys.** 2 species. Large game birds with bare skin on head and neck. |
| **Grouse.** 17 species. Plump birds with short, rounded wings. |
| **Pheasants and quails.** 186 species. Plump, often colourfully plumaged game birds. |

# Ostrich

The world's largest living bird, the ostrich is too big and heavy to fly. Instead it runs fast and can reach speeds of up to 70 kilometres an hour when fleeing from its enemies. Ostriches feed on plants and seeds but sometimes also catch small reptiles to eat. Ostrich eggs are larger than those laid by any other bird. One ostrich egg weighs about 1.5 kilograms – more than 18 times as much as a hen's egg.

FOUND IN:
**Africa**

SIZE:
**1.8–2.7 m tall**

SCIENTIFIC NAME:
**Struthio camelus**

# Brown kiwi

Using its long, sensitive beak, the brown kiwi probes in the undergrowth for insects and worms. Its keen senses of smell and hearing help it find food. Like other kiwis, this bird cannot fly.

FOUND IN:
**New Zealand**

SIZE:
**69 cm long**

SCIENTIFIC NAME:
**Apteryx australis**

# Emu

FOUND IN:
**Australia**

SIZE:
**2 m tall**

SCIENTIFIC NAME:
**Dromaius novaehollandiae**

# Great tinamou

Dense rainforest is the home of the great tinamou. It can fly but spends most of its time on the ground eating berries, seeds and insects.

FOUND IN:
**South America**

SIZE:
**45 cm long**

SCIENTIFIC NAME:
**Tinamus major**

# Common cassowary

The common cassowary lives in the tropical rainforest. It cannot fly and scientists think it may use the large horn casque, located on the top of its head, to help it break through the undergrowth as it searches for fallen fruits to eat. Males and females look similar, but females are slightly larger and have brighter plumage.

FOUND IN:
**New Guinea and northern Australia**

SIZE:
**1.5 m tall**

SCIENTIFIC NAME:
**Casuarius casuarius**

The emu is the second largest bird in the world and, like the ostrich, it cannot fly. It runs fast on its long legs, however, as it looks for food in the Australian bush. Fruit, berries and insects are the main foods of the emu, and it also eats grass and other crops.

# Greater rhea

The largest birds in South America, greater rheas are fast runners but cannot fly. They usually live in groups of up to 30 birds and eat plants, seeds, insects and small animals. At breeding time the male rhea mates with several females. He makes a shallow nest on the ground and incubates all of their eggs together.

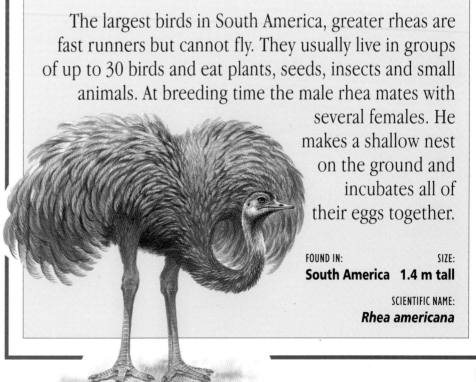

FOUND IN:
**South America**

SIZE:
**1.4 m tall**

SCIENTIFIC NAME:
**Rhea americana**

# FOCUS ON: *Grouse*

Grouse are plump birds, which look something like chickens. They live in the forests, moorlands and tundra of northern Europe, Asia and North America. There are about 16 kinds – birds such as the sage, ruffed and black grouse, the prairie chicken and the capercaillie. They range in size from about 30 to 90 centimetres long and most have brown, grey or black plumage.

All grouse can fly, but they spend much of their lives on the ground. They feed mostly on plants, particularly conifer needles and berries, but also catch insects and other small creatures in spring and summer.

Many kinds of grouse are famous for their courtship displays. In spring, the male birds compete for mates by performing group displays, called leks, on special areas of open land that are used every year. Day after day, the males puff themselves up, fan their feathers and stamp their feet in courtship dances. Weaker birds get tired and gradually drop out of the contest. The strongest, most experienced birds work their way to the centre of the group, where the leading males display. Female grouse gather to watch and mate with the leading males. After mating, the female grouse makes a nest, which is just a shallow hollow scraped in the ground.

**The ptarmigan's winter camouflage**
*In summer, the ptarmigan has mottled brown and grey feathers. But in autumn, the bird moults and grows plumage that is pure white, except for some black tail feathers. This white winter coat helps the ptarmigan hide from predators in its snowy Arctic home.*

### The magnificent sage grouse

One of the largest grouse, the sage grouse lives in North America. The male bird performs a spectacular courtship display. First, it raises its tail, spreads the feathers like a fan and puffs up the skin patches on its breast. Then it struts around, sometimes beating its wings, quivering its tail and making grunting sounds.

### Drumming display

The handsome male ruffed grouse attracts a mate by beating his wings to produce a drumming sound. At the same time, he raises his head crest, fluffs out his neck ruff and fans out his tail.

Female sage grouse

### Bird of moorland and tundra

The willow grouse, also known as the willow ptarmigan, roams tundra and heather-covered moorland. It eats the catkins of willow and birch trees and the shoots and berries of other tundra plants.

# Turkey

The wild turkey has a slimmer body and longer legs than domestic farm turkeys. It can fly well for short distances but finds most of its food on the ground. It eats seeds, nuts and berries and also catches small creatures, such as insects and lizards.

FOUND IN: **U.S. and Mexico**
SIZE: **90–120 cm long**
SCIENTIFIC NAME: *Meleagris gallopavo*

# Peafowl

The male peafowl (peacock) is one of the most magnificent of all birds. It has colourful feathers, and its glittering train, adorned with "eyespot" markings, can be spread by raising the tail beneath. With his train fanned out, the male struts around to attract the plainer female (peahen). Peafowl are featured in parks all over the world. They feed on seeds, grain, leaves and insects.

# Satin bowerbird

The male bowerbird builds a "bower" (chamber) on the ground to attract females. The bower is made of sticks and decorated with blue flowers and berries.

FOUND IN: **Eastern Australia**
SIZE: **30 cm long**

SCIENTIFIC NAME: *Ptilonorhynchus violaceus*

Male

Female

# California quail

California quail move and feed in flocks, eating leaves, berries and seeds. Both males and females have an unusual head plume.

FOUND IN: **Western U.S.**
SIZE: **23–28 cm long**

SCIENTIFIC NAME: *Lophortyx californica*

# Pheasant

FOUND IN: **Asia**
SIZE: **Male up to 90 cm long; female up to 60 cm**

SCIENTIFIC NAME: *Phasianus colchicus*

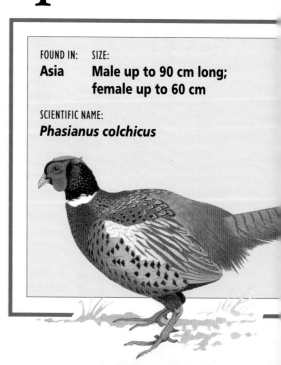

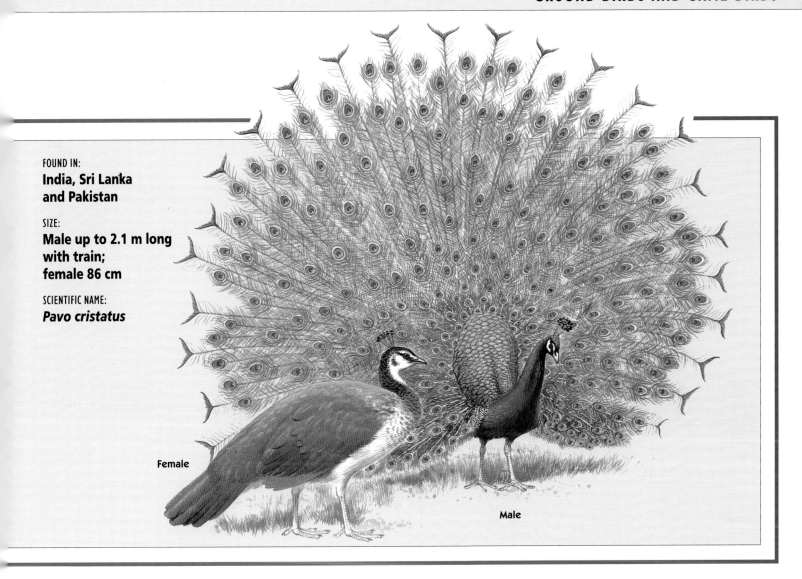

FOUND IN:
**India, Sri Lanka
and Pakistan**

SIZE:
**Male up to 2.1 m long
with train;
female 86 cm**

SCIENTIFIC NAME:
***Pavo cristatus***

**Female**

**Male**

# Junglefowl

Pheasants originally came
from Asia but have now
been introduced into
many other countries.
Wild pheasants
live in woodland
and grassland. They
spend much of their lives
on the ground eating
seeds, buds and berries.

The colourful junglefowl is
the ancestor of domestic
chickens. The female is
smaller and has brownish
feathers. Junglefowl move
in flocks of about 50 birds,
searching for grain, seeds
and insects to eat.

FOUND IN:
**Southeast Asia**

SIZE:
**Male 63–75 cm long; female 40–45 cm**

SCIENTIFIC NAME:
***Gallus gallus***

# Malleefowl

The malleefowl incubates its eggs in a mound of leaves and soil. As the leaves rot, the inside of the mound becomes very warm. The male keeps checking the temperature and removes material if it becomes too hot. When the young hatch, they dig their own way out of the mound.

FOUND IN:
**Southern Australia**

SIZE:
**53–60 cm long**

SCIENTIFIC NAME:
**Leipoa ocellata**

# Greater roadrunner

FOUND IN:
**Southwestern U.S. and Mexico**

SIZE:
**50–60 cm long**

SCIENTIFIC NAME:
**Geococcyx californianus**

True to its name, the greater roadrunner runs at speeds of up to 20 kilometres an hour on its big, strong feet. It can fly but does not often do so. This speedy bird lives in dry, open places and eats ground-living insects, such as crickets and grasshoppers, as well as birds' eggs, lizards and even snakes.

# Pallas's sandgrouse

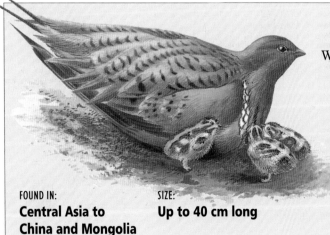

FOUND IN:
**Central Asia to China and Mongolia**

SIZE:
**Up to 40 cm long**

SCIENTIFIC NAME:
**Syrrhaptes paradoxus**

Pallas's sandgrouse lives on dry plains where water is hard to come by, and the male bird often flies long distances to find water for his chicks. On his belly are special feathers, which soak up water like little sponges. Once he finds a water hole, the sandgrouse wades in to soak his belly feathers. He then flies back to the nest where the chicks eagerly drink the water. Sandgrouse feed mostly on small dry seeds but sometimes they catch insects and other small creatures.

# *G*reat bustard

**FOUND IN:**
Parts of south and central Europe, across Asia to Japan

**SIZE:**
Male up to 104 cm long; female 75 cm

**SCIENTIFIC NAME:**
*Otis tarda*

The great bustard is one of the world's heaviest flying birds. A large male weighs up to 18 kilograms but can still manage to take flight. Females are much lighter – they weigh only up to 5 kilograms – and do not have bristly "whiskers". Great bustards move in flocks as they search for plants, seeds and insects to eat. They lay their eggs in a simple nest scraped in the ground.

# *G*reat curassow

The great curassow is a rainforest bird. It finds much of its food, such as fruit and leaves, on the ground but flies up into the trees to roost. If in danger, it runs away rather than flies. In the breeding season the curassow makes a nest of twigs and leaves in a bush or tree. The male has a loud booming call that is used to attract females and to warn off other males. The great curassow is very sensitive to disturbance and is one of the first birds to disappear when humans begin any activity in the forest. It has long been hunted and is now extremely rare.

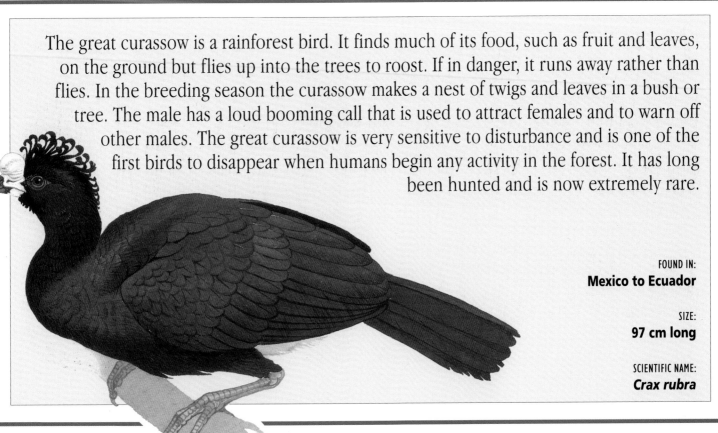

**FOUND IN:**
Mexico to Ecuador

**SIZE:**
97 cm long

**SCIENTIFIC NAME:**
*Crax rubra*

# Seabirds

*In the air, on the seas and under water, seabirds are among the most remarkable of all birds.*

Nearly 70 per cent of the earth's surface is covered by the oceans and seas, but only 3 per cent of all birds are seabirds. This is not surprising, considering how harsh and demanding a marine existence is. Many seabirds, such as albatrosses, terns and gannets, are powerful fliers and cover long distances over the open ocean as they search for food. Some spend almost the entire year in the air, only coming to land to breed, lay eggs and raise their chicks. There are some seabirds that cannot fly at all, however. Penguins are the best-known examples.

Just as several kinds of bird may live in the same habitat on land, different types of seabird can exist together in the same areas because they do not compete for the same food. For example, the shag and the great cormorant hunt for food in the North Atlantic Ocean at the same time of year. The shag eats mainly sand eels and herrings, which it catches in the open sea, while the cormorant eats shrimps and flatfish, which it finds on the seabed in shallow waters.

Most seabirds are excellent swimmers and some are superb divers. Their feathers form a dense, waterproof cover to protect them from the cold and wet. Chicks usually have a softer, downy plumage when they first hatch and develop their waterproof feathers only after several weeks or months.

*Gannets nest in noisy colonies of thousands of birds on rocks and islands. Birds usually return to the same nest sites year after year.*

# How seabirds live

**Gannet** plunging almost vertically into the sea from as high as 30 metres above the surface.

**M**any seabirds can swim and dive to perfection. Some, such as terns and gannets, dive out of the sky into the water to catch fish, while others, including puffins, plunge into the water from the surface. Cormorants chase fish under water until they are near enough to catch them in their hooked beaks. Still others float on the water feeding on tiny sea creatures called plankton and on debris from ships.

Not all seabirds swim and dive to get food. Some birds from the storm petrel family simply swoop down from the air and skim close to the water's surface to catch prey.

Gannets and tropicbirds are among the many seabirds that make their nests on cliff ledges and rocks on coasts or islands. Most lay one to three eggs. The young are helpless when they hatch and are cared for by both parents until they are able to fly. Many petrels and shearwaters nest in crevices on cliffs or in burrows, which they dig with their beaks and feet.

Some kinds of cormorant and pelican spend part of the year on freshwater rivers and lakes. They may breed and lay their eggs there, then migrate back to the sea for the rest of the time.

**Skimmer** flying along the surface of the sea, ready to scoop up prey.

**Gull** attempting to defend itself and its prey from an attacking skua.

**Penguin** diving under water and steering with its flippers.

**Cormorant** diving under water.

## Beaks

Seabirds have different shaped beaks according to what food they eat and how they catch it. Gannets and terns, which dive headfirst into the water, have straight, sharp beaks for cutting through the water and seizing their prey. Underwater hunters, such as penguins, also have straight beaks. The hooked beak of the petrel would not suit a diving bird but is good for holding on to wriggling prey and for tearing prey apart. The puffin can carry lots of fish back to land in its broad beak.

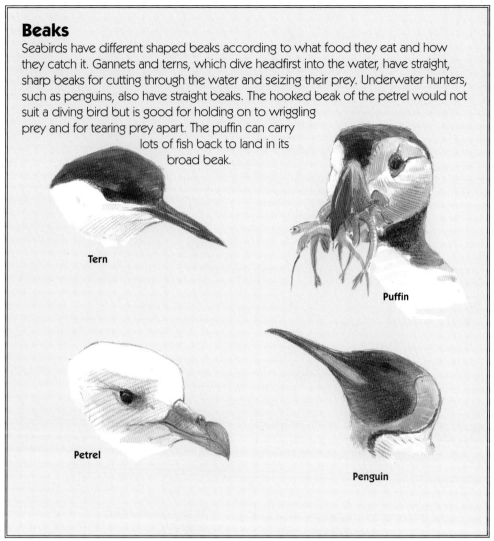

**Tern**

**Puffin**

**Petrel**

**Penguin**

| MAIN FAMILIES OF SEABIRDS |
| :---: |
| **Penguins.** 18 species. Flightless, sea-living birds with paddle-like wings. |
| **Albatrosses.** 14 species. Large birds which fly over open ocean on their long wings. |
| **Shearwaters and petrels.** 72 species. Short-tailed, slender-winged birds, which fly over open ocean. |
| **Storm petrels.** 20 species. Small birds that fly over open ocean. |
| **Tropicbirds.** 3 species. Elegant birds with long tail feathers. |
| **Gannets and boobies.** 9 species. Plunge-diving seabirds. |
| **Cormorants.** 32 species. Fish-eating birds that dive under water. |
| **Gulls.** 47 species. Heavy-bodied, long-winged coastal birds. |
| **Terns.** 41 species. Slender birds, with long, pointed wings and forked tails. |
| **Auks.** 22 species. Short-necked diving birds. |

**Storm petrel** "pattering" – bouncing over the sea with its feet touching the water as it feeds at the surface.

## Webbed feet

A web, or flap of skin stretched between the toes, allows seabirds, such as penguins, to use their feet like paddles. The web makes walking on land more difficult, however, and some seabirds tend to waddle.

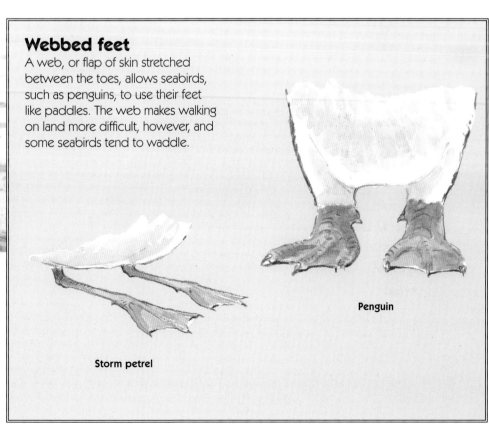

**Storm petrel**

**Penguin**

# Storm petrel

The storm petrel feeds mainly on fish and squid, which it catches as it swoops low over the water, as well as food scraps thrown from ships as rubbish. The storm petrel spends most of its life at sea but comes to land in the breeding season to nest in a burrow or rock crevice.

FOUND IN:
**Northeast Atlantic Ocean**

SIZE:
**13–18 cm long**

SCIENTIFIC NAME:
**Hydrobates pelagicus**

# Herring gull

This widespread gull scavenges on waste as well as catching fish. It also flies inland to find food on farmland.

FOUND IN:
**Most of Northern Hemisphere**

SIZE:
**53–65 cm long**

SCIENTIFIC NAME:
**Larus argentatus**

# Great skua

A strong bird with a hooked bill, the great skua is a fierce hunter. It not only attacks other birds to steal their prey, but also kills and eats puffins, kittiwakes and gulls, and preys on their eggs and young at breeding grounds. Unwanted fish thrown overboard from fishing boats are another source of food. The great skua nests in colonies, laying eggs in shallow nests it scrapes on the ground.

FOUND IN:
**North Atlantic Ocean**

SIZE:
**50–65 cm long**

SCIENTIFIC NAME:
**Catharacta skua**

# Wandering albatross

This graceful seabird has longer wings than any other bird – its wingspan measures up to 3.4 metres. The wandering albatross spends most of its life soaring over the open ocean, sometimes flying up to 500 kilometres in a day. It alights on the sea to seize fish and squid in its strong beak or to feed on rubbish from ships. It comes to land only to nest and rear its young. The female lays one egg, which is incubated by both parents.

FOUND IN:
**Southern oceans**

SIZE:
**1–1.4 m long**

SCIENTIFIC NAME:
**Diomedea exulans**

# Atlantic puffin

This puffin uses its colourful beak to catch fish and can hold as many as a dozen fish at a time. An expert swimmer and diver, the puffin can also fly well. It comes to land to nest and lay eggs.

FOUND IN:
**North Atlantic Ocean**

SIZE:
**28–30 cm long**

SCIENTIFIC NAME:
**Fratercula arctica**

# Common tern

FOUND IN:
**Northern coasts**

SIZE:
**33–40 cm long**

SCIENTIFIC NAME:
**Sterna hirundo**

A common coastal bird, this tern feeds on shrimps and other small sea creatures. It catches its food by hovering above the sea until it spots something, then diving rapidly into the water to seize the prey in its sharp beak.

# FOCUS ON: *Penguins*

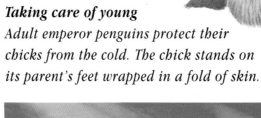

Penguins cannot fly but are better suited to life in the sea than any other bird. Expert swimmers and divers, they use their strong flippers to push themselves through the water and their webbed feet and tail for steering. On land, penguins walk upright and have an awkward gait.

Most penguins live around the Antarctic and on islands near the Antarctic Circle and have to survive in freezing conditions. They have a dense covering of glossy waterproof feathers, which keep them both warm and dry. A thick layer of fat beneath the feathers also helps to keep out the cold.

There are about 18 different kinds of penguin. The smallest is the little, or fairy, penguin, which is about 40 centimetres long. The biggest is the emperor penguin, which stands about 115 centimetres high. All look very similar, with black or blue-grey feathers on the back and white on the belly. Some have crests or coloured bands around the neck and head area. Male and female penguins look alike.

**Taking care of young**
*Adult emperor penguins protect their chicks from the cold. The chick stands on its parent's feet wrapped in a fold of skin.*

**Friendly behaviour**
*Penguins are sociable birds and when a pair meets, they rub their heads in greeting. Penguins also preen one another's feathers.*

### Tobogganing

Not at their best on land, penguins slip and slide as they waddle over the frozen ground. Often the birds lie down on their bellies and toboggan over the ice – a quicker and easier way to move. Once in the water, most penguins swim at speeds of 5–10 kilometres an hour.

### Antarctic nesters

Adélie penguins nest in huge colonies around the Antarctic coast. The birds return to the same sites year after year and often to the same mates.

### Underwater hunter

The king penguin dives deep for prey, such as squid, and often plunges to 45 metres or more. The deepest recorded dive for a king penguin is 250 metres.

# Red-tailed tropicbird

This elegant seabird is an expert in the air, but it moves awkwardly on land. It usually nests on ledges or cliffs in a position that allows for easy take-off. Fish and squid are the red-tailed tropicbird's main foods.

FOUND IN:
**Indian and Pacific Oceans**

SIZE:
**90–100 cm long including tail**

SCIENTIFIC NAME:
**Phaethon rubricauda**

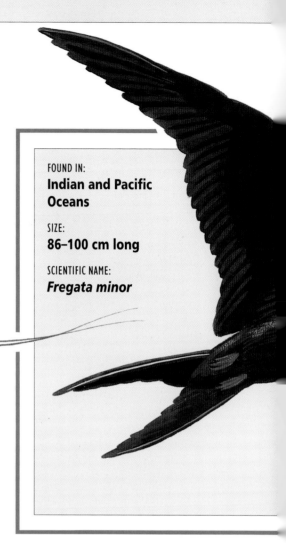

FOUND IN:
**Indian and Pacific Oceans**

SIZE:
**86–100 cm long**

SCIENTIFIC NAME:
**Fregata minor**

# Cormorant

The cormorant swims by using its webbed feet to push itself along. It eats mainly fish and catches prey during underwater dives that may last a minute or more. The cormorant usually brings fish to the surface and tosses them in the air so they can be swallowed headfirst.

FOUND IN:
**Coasts of North America, Europe, Africa, Asia and Australia**

SIZE:
**80–100 cm long**

SCIENTIFIC NAME:
**Phalacrocorax carbo**

# Northern gannet

A sturdily built seabird with a strong beak, the northern gannet soars over the ocean, searching for fish and squid. When it spots prey, the gannet will plunge 30 metres or more into the water to seize the catch and bring it to the surface.

# Great frigatebird

This large seabird has a wingspan of more than 1.8 metres and a big, hooked beak. It spends most of its life in the air and does not often land on the water. It catches food by snatching prey from the surface of the water or by threatening other seabirds until they drop their meals.

# Brown pelican

FOUND IN:
**Pacific and Atlantic coasts of North and South America**

SIZE:
**110–137 cm long**

SCIENTIFIC NAME:
**Pelecanus occidentalis**

The brown pelican feeds by diving for fish. It plunges into the water from heights of more than 9 mctres. As it enters the water, the pelican opens its mouth and catches the fish in the pouch below its beak.

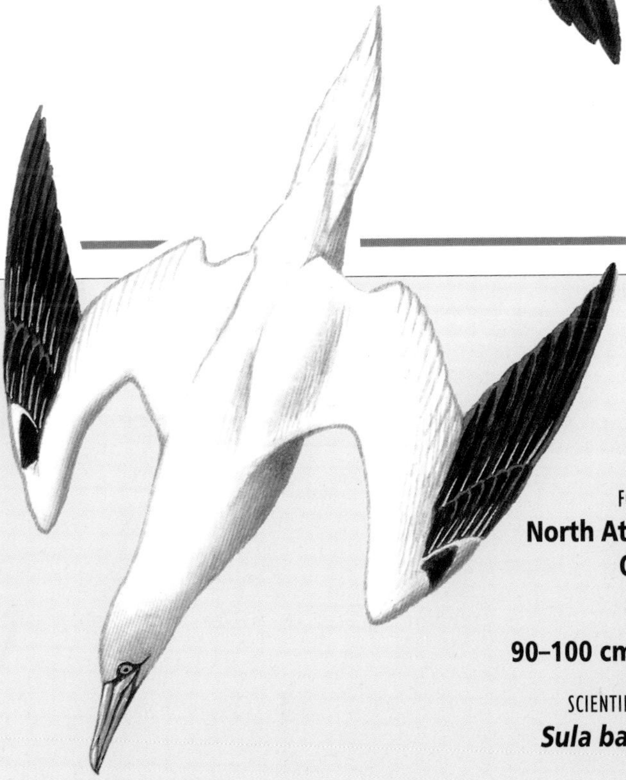

FOUND IN:
**North Atlantic Ocean**

SIZE:
**90–100 cm long**

SCIENTIFIC NAME:
**Sula bassana**

# Jackass penguin

The jackass penguin lives in a warmer climate than most other penguins. It comes to land to breed and nests in a burrow to avoid the hot African sun.

FOUND IN:
**Coasts of South Africa**

SIZE:
**69 cm long**

SCIENTIFIC NAME:
**Spheniscus demersus**

# Waterbirds and cranes

*Birds as varied as brilliantly patterned ducks and long-legged herons and flamingos live on the world's fresh waters.*

A huge variety of birds live in and around freshwater lakes, ponds, rivers and marshland. All of these habitats are rich in both plant and animal foods for birds, and there is usually plenty of shelter among bankside reeds and plants where birds can hide and nest.

One major group of waterbirds includes species such as egrets, storks, ibises and flamingos. Typically, these are large birds with long necks and legs that stand in water while feeding. Herons and egrets catch their prey in their sharp beaks, while flamingos feed on tiny water creatures and plants, which they filter from the water with their specially adapted beaks.

Ducks, geese and swans swim on the water as they look for food, and some even dive beneath the surface. Most have strong legs and webbed feet to help them swim. They nest on the ground, and the young are able to walk about and even swim within hours of hatching. A few types of duck, such as eiders and mergansers, are also found on coastal waters.

Other birds found in fresh water include cranes, grebes and divers, or loons. Cranes are long-legged birds that wade in shallow water to find food. Grebes and divers are fast swimmers that feed mainly on fish, which they chase and catch under water with their pointed beaks.

*Rosy-tinted flamingos gather on large lakes in spectacular flocks of as many as two million birds.*

# How *waterbirds and cranes live*

Birds of the heron family, which includes egrets and bitterns, hunt prey with their powerful, dagger-shaped beaks. The bittern, for example, moves slowly through marshland or shallow water, with its beak always ready to spear fish, crabs or frogs. The black heron has a strange feeding method. It stands in shallow water with its head down and its wings spread in a circle to form a canopy over its head. The resulting patch of shade may make it easier for the bird to see prey in the water and may even attract fish to the area.

Other waterbirds hold their beaks plunged in water as they feed. The wood stork wades along, moving its open beak from side to side. If its beak meets some prey, the bird snaps it shut.

Many waterbirds perform spectacular displays to court mates or warn off rivals. Great crested grebes have a long ritual during which both partners wag their heads, display head plumes and exchange gifts of pond weed.

Cranes, and their relatives trumpeters, also perform courtship dances in the breeding season to attract mates. The crowned crane is particularly dramatic as it stretches out its wings to display its feathers and leaps into the air.

**White stork** clattering its beak as it threatens a rival.

**Bittern** watching and waiting to stab prey with its beak.

## Feet

Swimming birds, such as ducks, have fully webbed feet, which they use like paddles to push them through the water. Storks, which wade in water and do not swim, have webs only at the base of their toes.

**Stork**

**Duck**

**Yellow-billed stork** feeding in water, moving its beak from side to side to search for prey.

**Great crested grebes** performing their intricate courtship display.

A crowned crane leaping into the air during its elaborate courtship dance.

## MAIN FAMILIES OF WATERBIRDS AND CRANES

**Herons and egrets.** 60 species. Long-legged birds, most with sharp, stabbing beaks.

**Storks.** 19 species. Long-necked, long-legged birds that feed on land and in water.

**Flamingos.** 5 species. Large birds, with very long legs, that feed in water.

**Ducks, geese and swans.** 147 species. Plump waterbirds with webbed feet and flattened beaks.

**Divers.** 4 species. Large waterbirds that dive for their food.

**Grebes.** 20 species. Medium to large diving birds.

**Cranes.** 15 species. Large, long-legged birds.

**Trumpeters.** 3 species. Forest birds related to cranes.

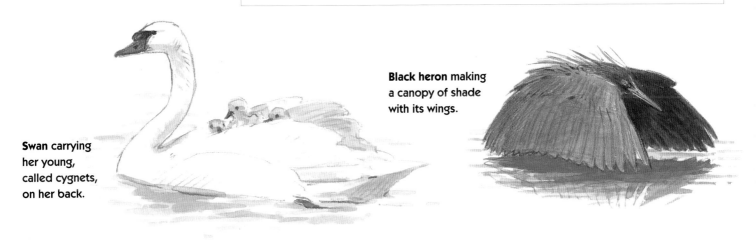

Swan carrying her young, called cygnets, on her back.

**Black heron** making a canopy of shade with its wings.

## Beaks

Geese have sharp-edged, wedge-shaped beaks, suitable for cropping grass and water plants. Most ducks have flattish beaks, suitable for snapping a variety of plant and animal food, but the merganser has a beak with serrated, saw-like edges, ideal for grasping fish. Herons, like storks, have sharp, straight beaks, ideal for catching fish.

**Goose**

**Heron**

**Merganser**

# Great white egret

This egret lives in marshy areas and eats fish, insects and other small creatures. It finds its food either by waiting in the water until it spots something or by stalking its prey. It makes its nest in a tree or clump of reeds.

FOUND IN:
**Worldwide**

SIZE:
**85–100 cm long**

SCIENTIFIC NAME:
*Egretta alba*

# Mallard

FOUND IN:
**Northern Hemisphere**

SIZE:
**50–63 cm long**

SCIENTIFIC NAME:
*Anas platyrhynchos*    Male    Female

The mallard is the ancestor of most domestic ducks. It has been introduced into Australia and New Zealand and can even live on ponds in city areas. It eats plants as well as insects, worms and other small creatures and is often seen feeding tail-up in shallow water. Females have brownish feathers and are plainer than the brightly coloured males.

# Tundra swan

This swan lays its eggs and rears its young on the Arctic tundra. In autumn, it migrates to warmer areas further south, usually returning to the same place year after year. Tundra swans feed on plants in shallow water.

FOUND IN:
**North America, northern Europe and Asia**

SIZE:
**1.2–1.5 m long**

SCIENTIFIC NAME:
*Cygnus columbianus*

# Greater flamingo

FOUND IN:
**Southern Europe, parts of Asia and Africa, Central and South America**

SIZE:
**124–145 cm long**

SCIENTIFIC NAME:
***Phoenicopterus ruber***

The flamingo's long legs allow it to wade into deeper water than most other birds when looking for food. It feeds by sucking water and mud in at the front of its beak and then pumping it out again at the sides, where bristly plates trap shrimps and other small water creatures.

# White stork

FOUND IN:
**Europe, Africa and Asia**

SIZE:
**100–114 cm long**

SCIENTIFIC NAME:
***Ciconia ciconia***

This long-legged bird eats frogs, reptiles, insects and snails. Storks often live near humans and will make nests on buildings as well as on trees and cliffs.

# Glossy ibis

FOUND IN:
**Central America, Africa, Eurasia and Australasia**

SIZE:
**55–65 cm long**

SCIENTIFIC NAME:
***Plegadis falcinellus***

The glossy ibis lives around lakes and in marshy areas. It eats insects and water creatures, which it picks from the mud with its long bill.

# Canada goose

This goose breeds in the north and migrates south in autumn. It eats both aquatic and land plants.

FOUND IN:
**North America**

SIZE:
**55–110 cm long**

SCIENTIFIC NAME:
***Branta canadensis***

**37**

# FOCUS ON: *Ducks*

Ducks belong to the waterfowl group, which also includes geese and swans. There are more than 120 different kinds of duck found all over the world, except in Antarctica. Ducks live in and around water – on coasts, or in freshwater lakes, rivers and swampland. A typical duck has a broad body, short legs and webbed feet. The beak is usually wide and slightly flattened, with tiny bristles called lamellae at the sides for straining food from the water. Underwater plants as well as insects, small fish and other water creatures, such as shrimps, are the ducks' main foods. Some ducks also eat plants and insects on land.

Most ducks are good swimmers and divers. Dabbling ducks, such as mallard and teal, feed on or just below the water's surface, with their heads down and tails in the air. Pochards and other diving ducks dive down below the surface to find food.

Ducklings hatch with a full covering of soft, downy feathers and their eyes open. They are able to swim and to feed themselves when only a day old.

**Shelduck in flight**
*The shelduck is a strong flier. It holds its neck stretched out and beats its wings powerfully, but more slowly than other ducks.*

**Staying with mother**
*Ducklings, such as these little pochards, are able to move around almost immediately after hatching, and it is important for them to stay close to their mother for protection. A duckling follows the first moving thing it sees after hatching – usually its mother – due to a rapid learning process called imprinting.*

**Shoveller**
*This duck is named after its broad, shovel-shaped beak. It uses this beak to filter seeds and tiny animals from the water.*

### Sea-living duck

The red-breasted merganser feeds on fish and lives in coastal seas as well as on lakes and rivers. Its long, slender beak has serrated edges similar to those of a bread knife, for grasping its slippery prey in water.

### Eider ducks

These ducks are strong fliers and spend much of their lives at sea and around coasts and islands. They dive in shallow water to feed on molluscs, such as mussels, which they scrape from rocks with their strong beaks.

### Upending for food

Ducks that feed on or just below the water's surface are called dabbling ducks. The duck plunges its head and front of its body into the water, leaving its tail sticking up in the air. In this position it eats seeds and small insects.

### Visitor from the east

The mandarin duck is from Asia but has now been introduced into parks in Europe. One of the most beautiful of all ducks, it performs an elaborate courtship display, using the sail-like feathers on its sides.

# Great crested grebe

FOUND IN:
**Europe, Asia, Africa, Australia and New Zealand**

SIZE:
**45–50 cm long**

SCIENTIFIC NAME:
**Podiceps cristatus**

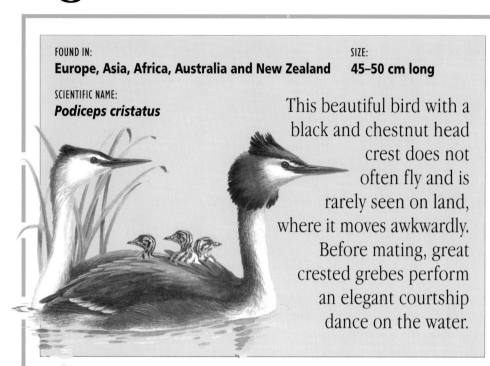

This beautiful bird with a black and chestnut head crest does not often fly and is rarely seen on land, where it moves awkwardly. Before mating, great crested grebes perform an elegant courtship dance on the water.

# Sunbittern

In its courtship display, the sunbittern lowers its neck, spreads its wings, and fans its tail to reveal colourful feathers.
Most of its life, though, is spent searching shallow water and wooded riverbanks for prey, including insects, frogs and small fish, which it seizes in its sharp beak.

# Red-throated diver

An expert swimmer, this bird feeds on fish, which it catches under water. It makes a variety of calls, including growling sounds and high-pitched wails.

FOUND IN:
**Northern Europe, Asia and North America**

SIZE:
**53–69 cm long**

SCIENTIFIC NAME:
**Gavia stellata**

# Moorhen

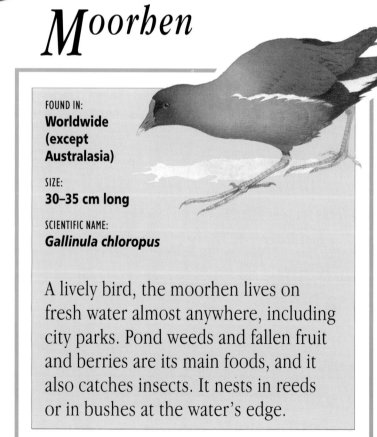

FOUND IN:
**Worldwide (except Australasia)**

SIZE:
**30–35 cm long**

SCIENTIFIC NAME:
**Gallinula chloropus**

A lively bird, the moorhen lives on fresh water almost anywhere, including city parks. Pond weeds and fallen fruit and berries are its main foods, and it also catches insects. It nests in reeds or in bushes at the water's edge.

# Common crane

Like other members of the crane family, the common crane is famous for its dancing display. The birds walk in circles, bowing, bobbing and tossing small objects over their heads. From time to time, they make graceful leaps in the air. Cranes nest on the ground or in shallow water. After breeding they journey south to spend the winter in northern Africa, India or Southeast Asia. Cranes migrate in large flocks, flying in V-formations with their long necks stretched out and legs trailing.

FOUND IN:
**Southern Mexico to Bolivia and Brazil**

SIZE:
**45 cm long**

SCIENTIFIC NAME:
**Eurypyga helias**

## Common trumpeter

A relative of the cranes, the common trumpeter lives in the Amazon rainforest. It rarely flies but can run fast on its long legs. Fruit, nuts and insects are its primary foods. When in flocks, the birds make the loud trumpeting calls which give them their name.

FOUND IN:
**South America**

SIZE:
**45–53 cm long**

SCIENTIFIC NAME:
**Psophia crepitans**

FOUND IN:
**Europe and Asia**

SIZE:
**110–120 cm long**

SCIENTIFIC NAME:
**Grus grus**

# Wading birds

*Flocks of wading birds gather to feed by rivers and on seacoasts all over the world.*

Also known as shorebirds, wading birds – such as sandpipers, plovers and jacanas – spend much of their lives on seacoasts and estuaries, or by rivers and lakes further inland. Most are small to medium sized, ranging from the smallest plovers, only 15 centimetres long, to curlews measuring almost 60 centimetres in length. Wading birds usually feed on the ground and most are fast runners. All are strong fliers, and many perform long migrations every year between winter feeding areas and the places where they lay eggs and rear young in spring and summer.

The sandpipers, which include birds such as whimbrels, snipes and woodcock, are found worldwide. Most have long, slender legs for wading in water and a long, often curved beak. Feathers are usually mottled browns and greys, which help the birds stay hidden on the ground. In winter, sandpipers feed mostly on creatures such as tiny snails and worms, which they dig from shores and marshy land with their sharp beaks. In summer, insects are a more important food.

Plovers, too, live all over the world. Most have shorter legs than the sandpipers and do not spend so much time in water. Plovers' beaks are usually straight and strong and the birds feed on insects, worms and small creatures such as crabs. Other wading birds include the avocets (which resemble sandpipers) oystercatchers and the long-toed jacanas.

*A bronze-winged jacana from India guards its nest on floating plants. The jacana's extraordinarily long toes allow it to walk delicately over leaves floating on the water.*

# How wading birds live

Wading birds, such as sandpipers and plovers, have beaks of various lengths and shapes for probing for food to different depths in mud and sand. The short-billed plovers feed at or near the water's surface. Many sandpipers, such as godwits and curlews, have much longer bills and can reach prey that lives in deep burrows. Another sandpiper, the common snipe, pushes its long, straight beak into water and soft mud, rhythmically pumping it up and down as it searches for small creatures to eat. Different types of wading bird may feed in the same areas but are not in competition with one another because each is adapted to catch a different range of prey.

One plover, the wrybill, has a unique beak, which bends to the right. The bird feeds by walking in circles, sweeping the tip of its bill over the mud with a scissoring action to pick up insects.

Wading birds usually make simple nests on the ground. The young are well developed when they hatch and most are able to move around and follow their parents to feeding areas within a day of hatching.

**Oystercatcher** in flight.

**Bar-tailed godwit** has a thin, slightly upturned beak, which it uses to dig for food.

**Grey plovers** search for worms, which live in burrows near to the ground's surface.

## Beaks

The wrybill is unique among birds in having a beak that curves to one side. A more typical wading bird is the curlew, with its long, slender beak. The avocet's beak curves upwards, and the bird moves its beak from side to side in the water or mud as it searches for food.

Curlew

Wrybill

Avocet

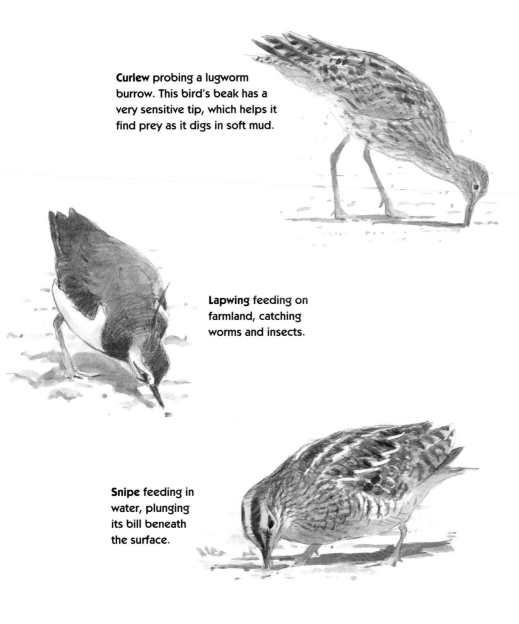

**Curlew** probing a lugworm burrow. This bird's beak has a very sensitive tip, which helps it find prey as it digs in soft mud.

**Lapwing** feeding on farmland, catching worms and insects.

**Snipe** feeding in water, plunging its bill beneath the surface.

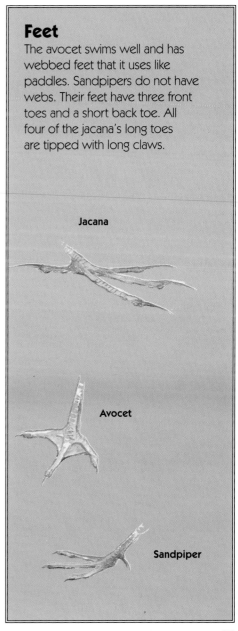

## Feet

The avocet swims well and has webbed feet that it uses like paddles. Sandpipers do not have webs. Their feet have three front toes and a short back toe. All four of the jacana's long toes are tipped with long claws.

Jacana

Avocet

Sandpiper

# Whimbrel

| FOUND IN: | SIZE: | SCIENTIFIC NAME: |
|---|---|---|
| **North America, Europe and Asia** | **38–43 cm long** | *Numenius phaeopus* |

The whimbrel breeds on the tundra of the far north. It then flies south for the winter. It uses its long beak to probe in the soil and mud for insects to eat.

# Redshank

This common bird lives near almost any kind of water. Insects are its main food, but it also eats other small creatures such as crabs and snails. It lays its eggs in a grass-lined nest made on the ground.

| FOUND IN: | SIZE: | SCIENTIFIC NAME: |
|---|---|---|
| **Europe and Russia** | **28 cm long** | *Tringa totanus* |

# American jacana

The jacana is best known for its extraordinary feet. The toes and claws are very long so that the bird's weight is spread over a large surface area. This allows the jacana to walk on unsteady surfaces, such as floating lily pads, as it searches for insects to eat.

| FOUND IN: | |
|---|---|
| **Southern U.S. and Central America** | |
| SIZE: | |
| **20–25 cm long** | |
| SCIENTIFIC NAME: | |
| *Jacana spinosa* | |

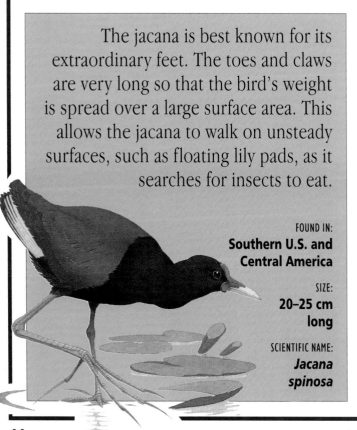

# Avocet

The avocet has an unusual beak that curves upwards. It catches insects and other small creatures by sweeping its beak from side to side in shallow water.

| FOUND IN: | SIZE: | SCIENTIFIC NAME: |
|---|---|---|
| **Europe and Asia** | **40–45 cm long** | *Recurvirostra avosetta* |

# Lapwing

The lapwing is also known as the "pee-wit" because of the shrill call it makes during its display flight. A common bird, able to live in many different kinds of area, it is often seen on farmland, damp meadows and marshes. It eats insects as well as worms, snails and some seeds. The lapwing lays its eggs in a shallow nest scraped on the ground. The female usually incubates the eggs, but the male often guards the nest. The young have mottled brown and white feathers. Alert to danger, they crouch down in the nest when they hear their parents' alarm calls.

FOUND IN:
**Europe and Asia**

SIZE:
**28–30 cm long**

SCIENTIFIC NAME:
***Vanellus vanellus***

# Common oystercatcher

The oystercatcher has a long, blunt bill that it uses to prise shellfish, such as cockles and mussels, off seashore rocks and to chisel them open. It also eats insects and worms, which it finds on farmland. It makes a nest on the ground and sometimes decorates it with stones or shells.

FOUND IN:
**Almost worldwide**

SIZE:
**45 cm long**

SCIENTIFIC NAME:
***Haematopus ostralegus***

# FOCUS ON: *Plovers*

More than 60 different kinds of plover live all over the world, roaming sandy and muddy shores, riverbanks and farmlands further inland. They range from 15 to 40 centimetres in length and most have plump, rounded bodies and short, straight beaks. The group includes birds such as lapwings, killdeers and dotterels as well as true plovers.

Plovers run fast and are strong fliers. Some, such as the American golden plover, make immensely long migrations, flying hundreds of kilometres south after breeding, then back again the following spring. Insects and other small creatures, such as worms and snails, are the plovers' main foods, but they also eat berries.

Typically, a plover lays its eggs in a nest that is little more than a shallow dip scraped in the ground. Both parents usually incubate the eggs and look after the young when they hatch.

## Tireless traveller

*The American golden plover is a champion long-distance traveller. It breeds on the Arctic tundra of North America and Siberia. After breeding, it flies approximately 13,000 kilometres south to spend the winter months in South America or Australia.*

## Fooling the enemy

*The killdeer, like several other birds, is well known for its "broken wing" display, which it performs if a predator comes near its nest. The killdeer walks away from the nest, trailing one wing as if it is injured. The predator follows, thinking it has found easy prey. Once the killdeer has led the enemy far enough away from its nest, it suddenly flies up and away.*

### Lapwings

In winter, lapwings usually feed near shores and estuaries, but in summer they fly inland to ploughed fields and other farmlands. Here, they probe the soil for worms and other small creatures.

### A threat display

Plovers often perform aggressive displays to warn off rivals. Here, a lapwing raises its wings to threaten another bird.

### Hiding from danger

Like all plovers, the Kentish plover nests on the ground. The young birds have mottled, brownish markings, which help them to stay hidden on stony, sandy ground. If they hear an alarm call from their parents, warning them of danger, the young birds flatten themselves on the ground, making themselves very hard to see.

### Wattled plover

The red flaps of skin, called wattles, near each eye give the wattled plover its name. These are shown off in the bird's courtship display.

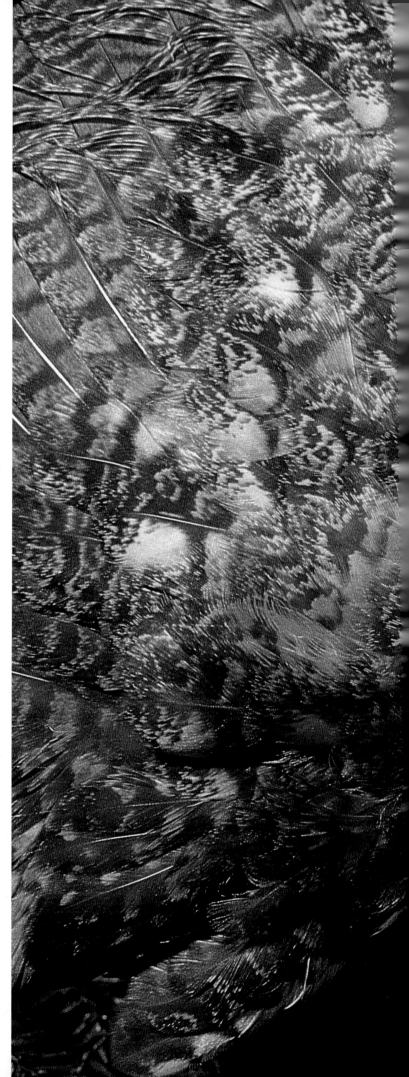

# Owls and birds of prey

*Powerful hunters such as eagles and owls are some of the fiercest, yet most magnificent, of all birds.*

Most birds of prey hunt and kill other creatures to eat. They are among the most exciting and interesting of all birds and include species such as eagles, hawks and buzzards. Although this is a varied group of birds, ranging from tiny falcons to huge harpy eagles and condors, all have features in common – keen vision, strong feet with sharp claws and a hooked beak for tearing prey apart.

Not all birds of prey are killers. Vultures are scavengers – they eat carrion, the bodies of creatures that are already dead. They soar over land on their long, broad wings searching for food. Some use their excellent sense of smell as well as their sight to find carrion.

Owls kill other birds and animals to eat, but unlike the hawks and eagles they usually hunt at night or at dawn and dusk. Most of the 130 or so kinds of owl look similar, with their large, disc-like faces and huge eyes. Typically, an owl sits on a branch watching and listening for the slightest movement of prey. When it hears something, it pinpoints the direction of the prey with its extraordinarily acute hearing before flying down to pounce. The edges of an owl's feathers are soft and fluffy – not hard like those of most birds. This cuts down the noise of flight so the deadly hunter can fly almost silently in the darkness.

*When alarmed or defending its nest, an owl spreads its wings and fluffs up its feathers to make itself appear larger and fiercer than it is.*

# How owls and birds of prey live

Birds of prey hunt in a variety of ways. Some, such as goshawks and sparrowhawks, usually live in forests and woodlands and hunt in the cover of trees. They move from one leafy perch to the next, ready to glide down swiftly to the ground to catch their prey in a sudden attack. Other birds of prey, such as buzzards and eagles, soar over open country, watching for victims. Some birds of prey have very specialized diets. The honey buzzard feeds mainly on bees and wasps and their young. It attacks nests to get at the insects and swallows some honey as it feeds.

Peregrine falcons are famed for their high-speed dives on to prey in mid-air, but not all falcons hunt in this way. Kestrels hover over the ground and if they see something, drop gently down on to it. The gyrfalcon catches its prey after a long chase near to the ground.

Owls are night-time hunters. Many watch for prey from a perch and then pounce, while others catch prey any way they can. Fishing owls fly over water and swoop down to the surface to seize fish with

**Barn owl** seizing a mouse with its strong claws.

their feet. Tiny, sharp spines on the soles of their toes help them grasp their slippery prey. Elf owls catch insects in the air, while burrowing owls hunt on the ground, catching mice and other small animals.

**Kestrel** hovering on fast-beating wings as it searches the ground for prey.

**Fish owl** plucks a fish from the water with its feet. Fish owls also eat crabs and small animals such as lizards and frogs.

| MAIN FAMILIES OF OWLS AND BIRDS OF PREY |
| --- |
| **Barn owls.** 14 species. Night-flying hunters with soft plumage and heart-shaped faces. |
| **Typical owls.** 160 species. Mostly night-flying hunters with soft plumage and saucer-shaped faces. |
| **New World vultures.** 7 species. Large, long-winged scavenging birds such as condors. |
| **Osprey.** 1 species. Fish-eating bird of prey. |
| **Eagles, hawks, buzzards.** 221 species. Small to large hunting birds with strong beaks and sharp claws. |
| **Falcons.** 57 species. Fast-flying hunters with long, pointed wings. |

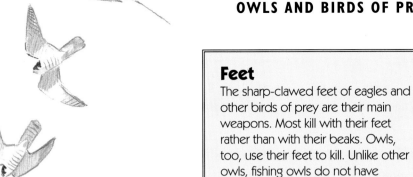

**Condor** circling over carrion. Condors are the largest of all the world's birds of prey. They soar for hours over mountains on their huge, outstretched wings.

**Peregrine falcon** making a high-speed dive, called a stoop, on to its prey, which it then catches in mid-air.

**Honey buzzard** attacking a bees' nest

## Feet

The sharp-clawed feet of eagles and other birds of prey are their main weapons. Most kill with their feet rather than with their beaks. Owls, too, use their feet to kill. Unlike other owls, fishing owls do not have feathered feet because their feathers would get wet and soiled with fish scales as they hunted.

Owl

Falcon

Condor

## Beaks

The upper part of the beak of a bird of prey, such as a buzzard, is hooked and pointed for tearing prey apart as it eats. Vultures, too, have strong beaks for cutting into the flesh of carrion. They also have unfeathered heads so that they can plunge into messy carcasses without soiling their plumage. An owl's beak is sharp but less powerful than a buzzard's.

Owl

Buzzard

Condor

# Barn owl

The barn owl is easily recognized by its pale, heart-shaped face. During the day it roosts in a sheltered spot, such as a barn or farm building or in a hole in a tree. At dusk it comes out to hunt for food, usually small creatures, such as rats and mice. This owl can find prey in almost total darkness, thanks to its extraordinarily good hearing.

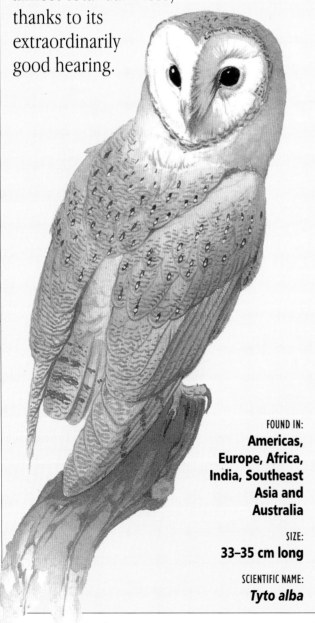

FOUND IN:
**Americas, Europe, Africa, India, Southeast Asia and Australia**

SIZE:
**33–35 cm long**

SCIENTIFIC NAME:
**Tyto alba**

# Lappet-faced vulture

Like all vultures, this bird feeds mostly on carrion – the bodies of animals that have died or been killed by predators. It has a strong, hooked beak and huge wings on which it soars searching for food.

| FOUND IN: | SIZE: | SCIENTIFIC NAME: |
| --- | --- | --- |
| **Africa and Middle East** | **100–104 cm long** | **Aegypius tracheliotus** |

# King vulture

FOUND IN:
**Mexico, Central and South America**

SIZE:
**75 cm long**

SCIENTIFIC NAME:
**Sarcorhamphus papa**

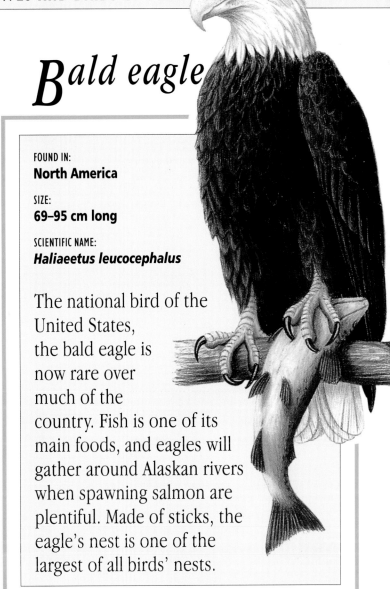

# *L*ong-eared owl

The tufts on the head of this owl are simply feathers and have nothing to do with the ears. But this bird does have excellent hearing, which helps it catch prey such as voles and mice.

FOUND IN:
**North America, Europe and Asia**

SIZE:
**33–40 cm long**

SCIENTIFIC NAME:
*Asio otus*

# *B*ald eagle

FOUND IN:
**North America**

SIZE:
**69–95 cm long**

SCIENTIFIC NAME:
*Haliaeetus leucocephalus*

The national bird of the United States, the bald eagle is now rare over much of the country. Fish is one of its main foods, and eagles will gather around Alaskan rivers when spawning salmon are plentiful. Made of sticks, the eagle's nest is one of the largest of all birds' nests.

With its brightly patterned head, the king vulture is one of the most colourful of all birds of prey. Although it may occasionally kill some prey for itself, it feeds mostly on carrion – animals that are already dead. Fish stranded on riverbanks are also an important source of food. The king vulture is one of the few birds that uses its sense of smell to find food.

# *S*nowy owl

The snowy owl hunts during the day, as well as at night, for prey such as hares and lemmings. The female is up to 20 per cent larger than the male and has dark markings on her feathers.

| FOUND IN: | SIZE: | SCIENTIFIC NAME: |
|---|---|---|
| **Arctic** | **53–65 cm long** | *Nyctea scandiaca* |

# Focus on: *Eagles*

Eagles are large birds of prey with strong, hooked beaks, sharp talons and big, golden eyes. They are fierce hunters that prey on other birds and animals. There are about 60 different kinds of eagle living all over the world.

Typically, a hunting eagle soars over the land on its broad wings for long periods, searching for food. With its keen eyesight, an eagle spots prey from a great distance, and then makes a rapid dive to the ground to seize and kill the animal with its talons. But some eagles hunt in a different way. Harpy eagles chase their prey through the trees, and sea eagles seize fish from the water.

Eagles usually build their nests in trees or on cliffs. The nests are made of sticks and branches and may be used year after year – but not always by the same birds. Nests can become very large as more twigs are added to them each time they are used. The biggest ever was a bald eagle's nest, which measured more than 6 metres in height.

**Food for the harpy**
*The harpy preys mostly on monkeys, sloths and tree porcupines.*

### Rainforest hunter

*The world's biggest and most powerful eagle, the harpy, lives in the South American rainforest. Instead of soaring high in the air, this eagle makes short flights from tree to tree, looking for prey. When it spots a victim, such as a monkey, the harpy chases it through the trees at high speed until it's close enough to catch the monkey in its strong talons.*

### A snake eagle

*Like other snake eagles, the crested serpent eagle feeds mostly on snakes and other reptiles. It sits in a tree to watch for prey then drops down on to it. The eagle's short, strong toes have a rough surface that helps it to grip wriggling prey.*

### The bald eagle

*With its glowing eyes and hooked beak, this magnificent bird is a typical bird of prey.*

### The sea eagle catching its prey

*Fish is the main food of the sea eagle. The bird soars over water looking for prey. It then swoops down to the surface to seize a fish in its talons. Sea eagles also catch other creatures and rob smaller birds of their catches.*

# Northern goshawk

A powerful, fast-moving hunter, the northern goshawk can catch creatures such as hares and pheasants. It kills its prey with its strong, sharp talons.

FOUND IN:
**North America, Europe and northern Asia**

SIZE:
**50–65 cm long**

SCIENTIFIC NAME:
**Accipiter gentilis**

# Osprey

This bird of prey feeds almost entirely on fish, circling up to 30 metres above water looking for food. When the bird catches sight of prey, it plunges down, throwing its feet forward to seize the fish. The soles of the osprey's feet are studded with small spines to help it grip its slippery catch.

FOUND IN:
**Almost worldwide**

SIZE:
**53–58 cm long**

SCIENTIFIC NAME:
**Pandion haliaetus**

# Rough-legged buzzard

The rough-legged buzzard hovers over the tundra as it hunts for prey, such as lemmings and voles. It nests in the far north, laying up to four eggs in a nest of twigs made in a tree or on a rocky ledge. After the breeding season, this buzzard flies south to spend the winter in a warmer climate.

FOUND IN:
**North America, northern Europe and Asia**

SIZE:
**50–60 cm long**

SCIENTIFIC NAME:
**Buteo lagopus**

# Red kite

FOUND IN:
**Europe, western Asia and northern Africa**

SIZE:
**60–65 cm long**

SCIENTIFIC NAME:
**Milvus milvus**

The red kite hunts in woodland and open country and often hovers briefly as it searches for prey, such as rats, birds and reptiles. Like vultures, it also eats carrion.

# Peregrine falcon

One of the fastest flying of all birds, the peregrine is an expert hunter that preys on other birds. It makes a spectacular high-speed dive towards its prey, often a pigeon or a dove, and seizes it in mid-air.

FOUND IN:
**Almost worldwide**

SIZE:
**38–50 cm long**

SCIENTIFIC NAME:
**Falco peregrinus**

# Golden eagle

The magnificent golden eagle has a hooked beak, extremely sharp eyes and strong feet with long curved claws. When hunting, the eagle soars over the land for long periods, patiently searching for food. Once it spots prey, it quickly dives down and kills its victim on the ground. Hares and rabbits are the eagle's main food, but it also catches birds such as grouse. Golden eagles make their nests high on a ledge or in a tree. The female usually lays two eggs, and her mate helps to feed and care for the chicks.

FOUND IN:
**North America, Europe, northern Asia and Africa**

SIZE:
**75–100 cm long**

SCIENTIFIC NAME:
**Aquila chrysaetos**

# Birds of the trees and masters of the air

---

*Many birds spend their lives high above the ground in trees or darting through the air in search of food.*

---

One of the many advantages of flight is that it allows birds to fly up into trees. There, among the branches, they find havens from ground-living hunters, as well as safe places to roost and make nests. Many birds also gather much of their food in trees. Pigeons and parrots feed mostly on the seeds, nuts and fruits of various trees. Others, such as woodpeckers and cuckoos, eat insects which they find on tree trunks and leaves. Bee-eaters and motmots perch on branches to watch for insects, then fly out to seize their prey in mid-air.

Some birds are more skilful fliers than others. Hummingbirds, for example, are true masters of the air and perform extraordinary aerial acrobatics. As they hover in front of flowers to feed, their wings beat more than 50 times a second – so fast that they can be seen only as a blur. Kingfishers, too, are experts in the air, darting and swooping at high speed as they search for prey.

Most birds return to a perch to eat their food, but swifts do almost everything, other than nesting, in the air. Their legs and feet are weak and they rarely, if ever, walk. Nightjars, too, eat in mid-flight. They fly with their beaks open, scooping up airborne insects such as moths.

---

*The brilliantly plumaged European kingfisher flies back to its perch after seizing a fish from the water.*

---

# How birds of the trees and masters of the air live

Many tree birds have beaks that are specially adapted to their particular way of finding food. The woodpecker, for example, uses its heavy, pointed beak for hammering into bark to get at the insects crawling beneath. Once it has made a hole in the bark, the woodpecker removes insects with its long, sticky-tipped tongue, which can be extended well beyond the tip of its beak. Toucans have large, colourful beaks, which may help them attract mates and also allow them to reach fruit at the ends of thin branches.

Trees make ideal nest sites. Helped by her mate, the female hornbill actually walls herself up inside her tree-hole nest while she incubates her eggs and cares for her young. Only when the young are big enough to fly does the male bird help her break open the nest.

Swifts are among the most agile birds in the air. Some experts believe that once a young swift leaves its nest, it does not come to land again until it is ready to breed, at about two years old. By then some swifts have flown as many as 500,000 kilometres. Because swifts have weak feet, they cannot perch and usually only land on vertical surfaces.

Toucan reaching for fruit with its large beak.

Nightjar flying with its wide beak open to catch insects.

Bee-eater snapping an insect from the air.

| MAIN FAMILIES OF BIRDS OF THE TREES AND MASTERS OF THE AIR |
| --- |
| **Pigeons.** 300 species. Plump, mainly tree-living birds. |
| **Parrots.** 340 species. Mostly tree-living birds with large, hooked beaks. |
| **Cuckoos.** 138 species. Woodland birds, some of which lay their eggs in other birds' nests. |
| **Hornbills.** 48 species. Medium to large birds with long beaks. |
| **Woodpeckers.** 199 species. Tree-living birds with strong, pointed beaks. |
| **Toucans.** 35 species. Medium to large birds with long, often brightly coloured, beaks. |
| **Kingfishers.** 92 species. Long-billed, fast-flying birds. |
| **Swifts.** 92 species. Long-winged, acrobatic fliers. |
| **Hummingbirds.** 334 species. Nectar-eating birds that can hover and fly backwards. |
| **Swallows.** 81 species. Expert fliers with long, pointed wings and forked tails. |

**Kingfisher** swooping down from its perch over a river to seize a fish from the water.

## Beaks

A parrot's strong, hooked beak is like a powerful nutcracker and can break even the hardest shells. A pigeon's beak is smaller, suited to picking up seeds and berries. The jacamar snaps insects out of the air with its long, pointed beak, while the swift has a shorter beak that it opens wide to capture flying insects.

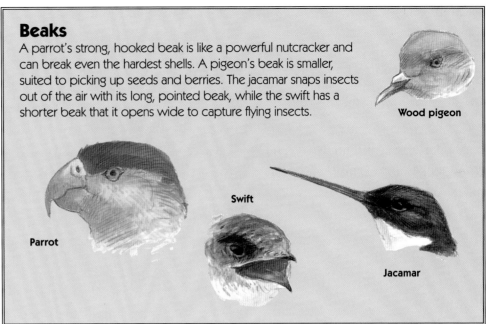

Wood pigeon

Parrot

Swift

Jacamar

**Cuckoo** laying its egg in another bird's nest. The cuckoo has to lay its egg very quickly before the owner of the nest returns.

**Woodpecker** hammering a tree trunk with its beak to extract insects from the bark.

## Feet

There is a wide variety of feet in this group. A swift has short legs and weak feet. Its toes are arranged in two pairs, two to the right and two to the left, which helps the bird cling to vertical surfaces. Kingfishers, too, have weak feet, with the second and third toes partly joined. Pigeons, like most birds, have three toes pointing forwards and one backwards, suitable for perching and walking. Woodpeckers and parrots are true tree-living birds. They have two toes pointing forwards and two backwards, giving them a sure grip.

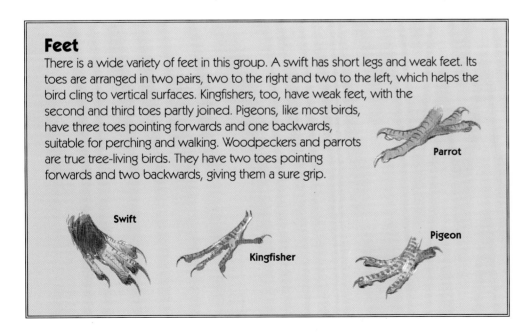

Parrot

Swift

Kingfisher

Pigeon

# Rainbow lorikeet

The pattern of the colourful feathers of the rainbow lorikeet varies slightly from bird to bird. The bird lives in rainforest and woodland and usually feeds high up in the trees. Screeching, chattering flocks fly among the branches, eating fruit, insects, pollen and nectar. At night they roost in huge groups of up to several thousand birds. Rainbow lorikeets nest in holes in trees. The female lays two or three eggs.

**FOUND IN:**
**Indonesia, New Guinea, northern and eastern Australia**

**SIZE:**
**28–30 cm long**

**SCIENTIFIC NAME:**
*Trichoglossus haematodus*

# Sulphur-crested cockatoo

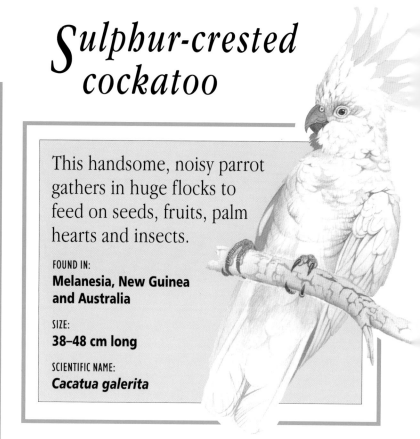

This handsome, noisy parrot gathers in huge flocks to feed on seeds, fruits, palm hearts and insects.

**FOUND IN:**
**Melanesia, New Guinea and Australia**

**SIZE:**
**38–48 cm long**

**SCIENTIFIC NAME:**
*Cacatua galerita*

# Victoria crowned pigeon

**FOUND IN:**
**New Guinea, Biak and Yapen Islands**

**SIZE:**
**65–75 cm long**

**SCIENTIFIC NAME:**
*Goura victoria*

# Rock dove

The rock dove is the ancestor of all city and domestic pigeons. Wild rock doves move in flocks or small groups and feed mainly on seeds. A mated pair makes a nest of twigs and grass on a cliff ledge or in a hole in a tree, cliff or building. The female lays two eggs.

FOUND IN:
**Europe, parts of Asia and northern Africa**

SIZE:
**30–33 cm long**

SCIENTIFIC NAME:
*Columba livia*

The world's largest pigeon, the Victoria crowned pigeon has been hunted heavily and is now rare. This beautiful bird usually feeds on the ground, eating fallen fruit, seeds and berries. If disturbed, it flies off to perch on a tree branch. A male bird defends his territory by opening one wing, ready to strike blows against any intruder. The large nest is made in a tree, and the female usually lays only one egg, which both parents incubate.

# Scarlet macaw

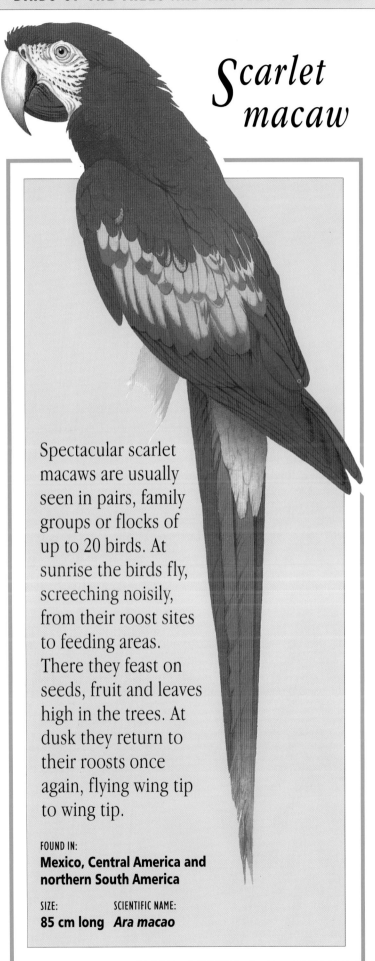

Spectacular scarlet macaws are usually seen in pairs, family groups or flocks of up to 20 birds. At sunrise the birds fly, screeching noisily, from their roost sites to feeding areas. There they feast on seeds, fruit and leaves high in the trees. At dusk they return to their roosts once again, flying wing tip to wing tip.

FOUND IN:
**Mexico, Central America and northern South America**

SIZE:
**85 cm long**

SCIENTIFIC NAME:
*Ara macao*

# FOCUS ON: *Parrots*

**Crimson rosella**
*This small parrot lives in the eucalyptus forests of Australia.*

Parrots are brightly coloured, tree-living birds. There are more than 300 different species in the family, including cockatoos, lories, macaws, lovebirds and parakeets. They live in tropical and subtropical areas of the Americas, Africa, Asia and Australia, usually in forests and woodlands.

Parrots are expert climbers. They have short, strong legs and feet, with two toes pointing forwards and two backwards – ideal for holding on tight to branches. Unlike any other birds, parrots also use their feet like hands for bringing food up to their beaks. Fruit and nuts are the main foods of parrots. They can crack even the hardest shelled nuts with their powerful beaks.

Most parrots gather in huge, noisy flocks, screeching and cackling as they fly to feeding sites. They pair for life, and both parents help to feed and care for the young. Sadly, many parrots are now rare. Large areas of their forest habitats have been destroyed or disturbed, and countless birds have been taken illegally for the pet trade.

**Rainbow lorikeet**
*Like all parrots, lorikeets are very sociable birds. Pairs preen each other for hours, removing ticks and lice.*

**An upside-down parrot**
*The blue-crowned hanging parrot gets its name from its strange habit of hanging upside down from a branch while resting at night or during the day. There are 10 other species of hanging parrot.*

**A flightless parrot**
*The kakapo of New Zealand is not like any other parrot. It cannot fly, lives on the ground and is active only at night. It is also the heaviest of all parrots. Kakapos are now extremely rare and live only on two small islands off the coast of New Zealand.*

**Hyacinth macaw**
With its long tail, this macaw is the largest of all parrots. It has what is probably the strongest beak of all birds.

**Eclectus parrot**
During the day, flocks of eclectus parrots fly through the forest looking for food. In the evening, they perform special display flights before gathering in groups of up to 80 birds and settling down for the night.

**Palm cockatoo**
The splendid palm cockatoo has interesting courtship habits. To attract the attention of females in the breeding season, the male bird holds a stick in his claws and pounds it against a tree trunk to make a loud drumming noise.

**Golden parakeet**
This little parakeet lives in the Brazilian rainforest where, despite its bright colours, it is surprisingly hard to see.

**Clay-eating macaw**
Like other macaws, the blue and yellow macaw often eats seeds containing substances that are poisonous or unpleasant-tasting to humans but do not appear to harm the macaws. The birds are also often seen eating clay at special sites called clay licks. Experts think that the clay may counter the effects of the poisons.

# Hoatzin

Although it lives in trees, the hoatzin is a poor flier. It glides from perch to perch and uses its wings for support as it clambers along branches. Fruit, buds and leaves are its main foods.

FOUND IN:
**South America: Amazon and Orinoco basins**

SIZE:
**60 cm long**

SCIENTIFIC NAME:
**Opisthocomus hoazin**

# Great Indian hornbill

FOUND IN:
**India, Southeast Asia and Sumatra**

SIZE:
**124–145 cm long**

SCIENTIFIC NAME:
**Buceros bicornis**

# Cuckoo

The cuckoo does not make its own nest but lays its eggs in the nests of other birds. The "foster parents" care for the young.

FOUND IN:
**Europe and Asia**

SIZE:
**33 cm long**

SCIENTIFIC NAME:
**Cuculus canorus**

# Red-crested turaco

A fruit-eating bird, the red-crested turaco lives in trees and does not often come down to the ground.

FOUND IN:
**Africa**

SIZE:
**40 cm long**

SCIENTIFIC NAME:
**Tauraco erythrolophus**

# *Q*uetzal

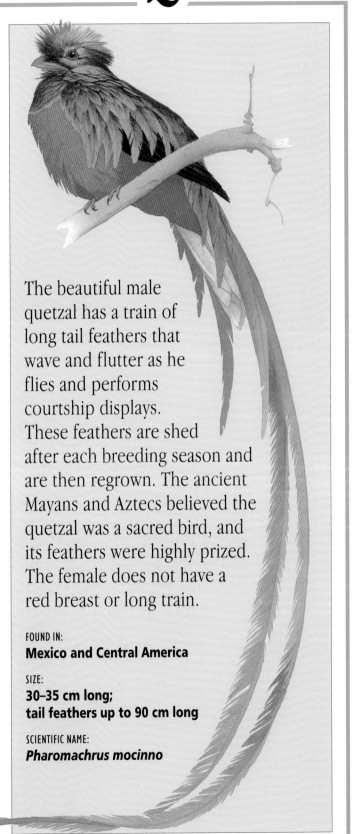

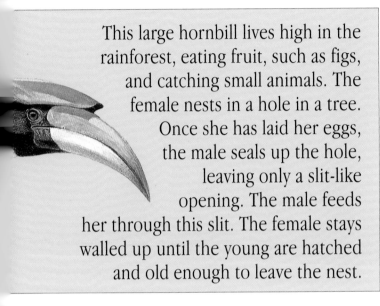

This large hornbill lives high in the rainforest, eating fruit, such as figs, and catching small animals. The female nests in a hole in a tree. Once she has laid her eggs, the male seals up the hole, leaving only a slit-like opening. The male feeds her through this slit. The female stays walled up until the young are hatched and old enough to leave the nest.

The beautiful male quetzal has a train of long tail feathers that wave and flutter as he flies and performs courtship displays. These feathers are shed after each breeding season and are then regrown. The ancient Mayans and Aztecs believed the quetzal was a sacred bird, and its feathers were highly prized. The female does not have a red breast or long train.

FOUND IN:
**Mexico and Central America**

SIZE:
**30–35 cm long;
tail feathers up to 90 cm long**

SCIENTIFIC NAME:
**Pharomachrus mocinno**

# *B*elted kingfisher

This kingfisher is an agile flier. It watches for prey from a tree overhanging a river or stream, then dives down to seize a fish or frog from the water.

FOUND IN:
**North America**

SIZE:
**30 cm long**

SCIENTIFIC NAME:
**Megaceryle alcyon**

# Blue-crowned motmot

With its tail swinging from side to side like a pendulum, the motmot sits watching for prey. It darts out from its perch to catch insects, spiders and lizards.

FOUND IN:
**Mexico, Central and South America**

SIZE:
**40 cm long**

SCIENTIFIC NAME:
**Momotus momota**

# Pileated woodpecker

Ants, termites and fruit are the main foods of this woodpecker. Clinging tightly to a tree trunk with its sharp claws, the bird hammers into the bark with its strong beak to find prey.

FOUND IN:
**North America**

SIZE:
**38–48 cm long**

SCIENTIFIC NAME:
**Dryocopus pileatus**

# Rufous-tailed jacamar

This long-billed bird catches its insect prey in mid-air. It then flies to a perch and bangs the insect against a branch to kill it before eating it.

FOUND IN:
**Mexico, Central and South America**

SIZE:
**23–28 cm long**

SCIENTIFIC NAME:
**Galbula ruficauda**

# Toco toucan

Although the toco toucan's colourful beak is up to 18 centimetres long, it is not solid, so it is not as heavy as it looks. Inside the largely hollow beak are criss-crossed rods of bone that give it strength. The toucan feeds mostly on fruit. It picks up food in the tip of its bill, then throws its head back and tosses the morsel into its mouth.

# Double-toothed barbet

This barbet perches in the shade of trees and bushes. It eats the fruit and nuts it finds in the trees or darts out to catch flying termites.

FOUND IN:
**Africa**

SIZE:
**23 cm long**

SCIENTIFIC NAME:
**Lybius bidentatus**

FOUND IN:
**Eastern South America**

SIZE:
**60 cm long**

SCIENTIFIC NAME:
**Ramphastos toco**

# Hoopoe

FOUND IN:
**Europe, Asia and Africa**

SIZE:
**28 cm long**

SCIENTIFIC NAME:
**Upupa epops**

This bird catches insects in trees and on the ground. It nests in a hole in a tree or wall. The female lays two to nine eggs and is fed by her mate as she incubates them.

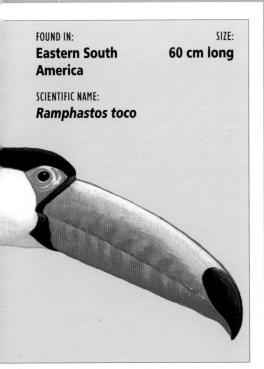

# European bee-eater

True to its name, this bird eats bees and wasps. It rubs its prey on a branch to destroy the sting and remove the venom before eating it.

FOUND IN:
**Europe, Asia and Africa**

SIZE:
**25–28 cm long**

SCIENTIFIC NAME:
**Merops apiaster**

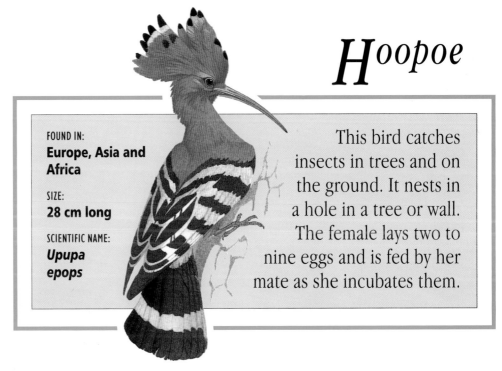

71

# FOCUS ON: *Hummingbirds*

Hummingbirds, named after the humming sound made by the rapid beating of their wings, are more agile in the air than any other birds. They can hover in front of flowers as they feed, wings moving so fast that they are almost invisible. Hummingbirds can fly upwards, sideways, downwards and even backwards.

Hummingbirds live only in North, Central and South America, mostly in the warmest parts. They measure from just over 5 centimetres to about 20 centimetres long, but the tail feathers make up as much as half of this length. Many have colourful, glittering plumage and decorative head crests and tail feathers. Females usually have duller feathers than males.

Flower nectar is the main food of hummingbirds. Most have long beaks, which they plunge deep into flowers to extract the nectar.

*Courtship display*

*This hummingbird, known as the marvellous spatuletail, has only four full-grown tail feathers, two of which have a long, bare shaft ending in a broad wedge shape, or spatule. During his courtship display, the male bird displays these decorative feathers as he flies to and fro in front of the female.*

### The longest beak

*The sword-billed has a longer beak than any other hummingbird. The beak allows the bird to reach nectar inside the deepest tube-shaped flowers. This bird also catches insects in the air.*

### Hovering hummingbird

*A brilliantly plumaged magenta-throated woodstar hovers as it takes nectar from a poinsettia flower.*

**A colourful hummingbird**
*The male crimson topaz is one of the most beautiful hummingbirds, with colourful plumage and long, curving tail feathers. It takes nectar from a wide range of flowers and also catches insects. The female bird has mostly green feathers.*

**White-tipped sicklebill**
*The strongly curved beak of the white-tipped sicklebill is perfect for taking nectar from flowers such as heliconias.*

**The smallest bird**
*The bee hummingbird is the world's tiniest bird. The male is only about 5 centimetres long, including its beak and tail. Females are about $1/2$ centimetre longer.*

# Ruby-throated hummingbird

Hummingbirds are named after the sound made by the rapid beating of their wings. Among the smallest of all birds, they can hover, fly upwards, sideways and even backwards with ease. Like all hummingbirds, the ruby-throated bird plunges its beak deep inside flowers to feed on nectar.

FOUND IN:
**North America**

SIZE:
**9 cm long**

SCIENTIFIC NAME:
**Archilochus colubris**

# Barn swallow

FOUND IN:
**Almost worldwide**

SIZE:
**18 cm long**

SCIENTIFIC NAME:
**Hirundo rustica**

The barn swallow eats insects, which it catches in the air or takes over water. It breeds during the summer in the northern hemisphere. Both male and female help to make a nest of mud and dead grass on the wall of a building, and the female lays four or five eggs. After breeding, the birds fly south to escape the northern winter.

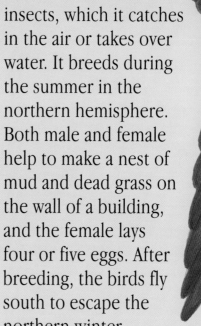

# Nightjar

By day, the nightjar perches quietly on a branch or on the ground, its mottled brown feathers helping it to stay hidden. At sunset, it takes to the air to dart after moths and other night-flying insects. The nightjar's tiny beak opens very wide and is fringed with bristles that help it to trap its prey. It makes its nest on the ground, and the female lays two eggs.

FOUND IN:
**Europe, Asia and northern Africa**

SIZE:
**28 cm long**

SCIENTIFIC NAME:
**Caprimulgus europaeus**

# Potoo

The potoo feeds by night, flying out from a perch to capture insects in its large beak. By day, it sits upright and very still on a broken branch or stump. With its head and beak pointing upwards, the potoo looks like part of the tree and so is hidden from its enemies.

FOUND IN:
**West Indies, Central America and tropical South America**

SIZE:
**35–40 cm long**

SCIENTIFIC NAME:
**Nyctibius griseus**

# White-throated swift

Swifts are fast and expert fliers. They catch insects, eat, drink and even mate in the air. Their legs and feet are tiny, and they rarely walk. The white-throated swift nests anywhere, from sea cliffs to ledges high in the mountains. The female lays as many as six eggs.

FOUND IN:
**Western U.S. and Central America**

SIZE:
**15–18 cm long**

SCIENTIFIC NAME:
**Aeronautes saxatilis**

# Poorwill

FOUND IN:
**North America**

SIZE:
**20 cm long**

SCIENTIFIC NAME:
**Phalaenoptilus nuttallii**

Named after its call, which sounds like "poor-will", this bird flits around at night, hunting moths and beetles. It is the only bird known to hibernate and each autumn it finds a rock crevice in which to spend the winter. Its body temperature falls and heart and breathing rates slow down, so that it uses as little energy as possible.

# Songbirds

---

*Their tuneful melodies make the
songbirds among the best loved
of all the world's birds.*

---

About half of all the kinds of bird in the world are
included in the group known as songbirds. While
not all sing as sweetly as the lark or the nightingale, the
males of most species are normally able to sing sequences
of musical notes. They sing when courting mates or
defending their territory. Female singers are rare, but
in a few species, such as song sparrows and robins,
female birds do sometimes sing.

Songbirds are also called perching birds and have
feet that are well adapted to their habit of perching on
trees and posts. Their feet have four toes – three that
point forwards and one backwards – and are ideally
shaped for holding on to twigs, reeds and even unnatural
perches such as wires. The toes are never webbed –
these are land birds although some may live near water.
Songbirds have few other features in common. Beaks
vary in shape according to the food eaten, and the birds
range in size from small species, such as tiny wrens and
finches measuring only a few centimetres, to ravens and
lyrebirds, which are more than 60 centimetres long.

There are more than 4,000 different kinds of songbirds.
They live all over the world, except at the Poles, in every
kind of habitat from deserts to rainforests and city
centres. Many have adapted well to life alongside humans
and have learned to feed on farmland, take food provided
in gardens and nest on buildings.

---

*The beautiful scissor-tailed flycatcher will
sit on a perch for hours, occasionally darting
out to capture flying insects.*

---

# How songbirds live

Within a group that ranges from tiny wrens to sturdy ravens there are birds with many different lifestyles. Insects, seeds, fruits and nectar are some of the main foods of songbirds. Some, such as finches, feed mainly on seeds. The goldfinch eats the tiny seeds of thistle and teasel heads with its thin, pointed beak. The crossbill feeds almost entirely on conifer seeds, which it extracts from pine cones. Other songbirds eat insects as well as nuts and seeds. Titmice, or chickadees, search for insects, seeds and berries in trees, often hanging upside down to peer into crevices or under leaves.

Insects are the main food of many songbirds, including antbirds and wrens. These little birds move stealthily through low bushes and plants catching grasshoppers, beetles and any other insects as

**Weaverbird** with its intricate nest that it weaves from thin grass strips and fixes to two or three upright grass stems. The entrance is a small hole in the side.

**Flycatcher** catching an insect in mid-air.

**Goldfinch** perched on a thistle feeding on its seeds. It also eats the seeds of other common weeds. The goldfinch has an attractive tinkling song.

**Sunbird** feeding on nectar. The bird uses its long beak to probe the flower for nectar and insects.

## Beaks

The crossbill's unusual beak, with its crossed tips, is shaped for removing seeds from pine cones. Starlings and antbirds have strong, straight beaks, suitable for catching insects or any other foods. The sunbird's beak is specially adapted for taking nectar from flowers.

**Crossbill**

**Antbird**

**Sunbird**

**Starling**

well as ants. For most sunbirds, however, sweet nectar is the most important food. They have long curving beaks for reaching deep into flowers for nectar. Thrushes, starlings and crows eat just about anything from fruit and berries to insects, snails, worms and larger prey such as lizards and frogs.

Songbirds have many different ways of making their nests, but all have young that hatch blind and helpless, with no feathers. Most songbirds care for their young for a number of weeks until they have a full covering of feathers and can fly.

**Blackbird pulling an earthworm from the ground. It also turns over leaf litter to uncover a variety of other small creatures. The blackbird has an attractive whistling song.**

**Skylark hovering in the air singing its song, which is made up of a series of melodious trills.**

**Wood warbler feeding its young in the nest it makes in the fork of a tree or bush.**

| MAIN FAMILIES OF SONGBIRDS |
|---|
| **Antbirds.** 246 species. Small, forest-dwelling birds, which usually feed on insects. |
| **Tyrant flycatchers.** 397 species. Small to medium birds, most of which catch insects in the air. |
| **Larks.** 81 species. Small, ground-feeding birds. |
| **Shrikes.** 69 species. Small to medium birds with hooked beaks. |
| **Wrens.** 69 species. Small, plump insect-eaters. |
| **Thrushes.** 329 species. Small to medium birds, many of which are common in gardens. |
| **Old World warblers.** 376 species. Small birds, usually found in trees or on grassland. |
| **Sunbirds.** 120 species. Small birds, often with long beaks and colourful plumage. |
| **Honeyeaters.** 170 species. Tree-living birds, which feed mostly on nectar. |
| **Buntings and sparrows.** 284 species. Small, mainly ground-living birds with strong feet for scratching for food. |
| **Tanagers.** 246 species. Small to medium, often brightly coloured birds. |
| **American orioles.** 96 species. Small to medium, usually black birds. |
| **Starlings.** 108 species. Lively, active birds with long, straight bills and strong legs. |
| **Birds of paradise.** 42 species. Forest birds; males have colourful plumage. |
| **Crows.** 113 species. The largest songbirds. |

## Feet

The songbirds all have four-toed feet, three toes facing forwards and one backwards, suitable for perching. The thrush and the chickadee are typical examples.

Chickadee

Thrush

# Long-billed woodcreeper

Using its long beak, this woodcreeper searches the leaves of rainforest plants for insects and spiders to eat. It is an expert climber and uses its stiff tail for support as it clambers around trees.

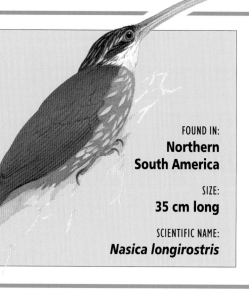

FOUND IN:
**Northern South America**

SIZE:
**35 cm long**

SCIENTIFIC NAME:
**Nasica longirostris**

# Rufous hornero

The rufous hornero searches for food on the ground, digging out earthworms and insects with its sharp beak. It builds an unusual, dome-shaped nest made of mud and straw. The female lays up to five eggs in a chamber inside the nest.

# Eastern kingbird

This noisy bird attacks anything that enters its territory, particularly larger birds. It eats insects.

FOUND IN:
**North America**

SIZE:
**20–23 cm long**

SCIENTIFIC NAME:
**Tyrannus tyrannus**

# Superb lyrebird

FOUND IN:
**Australia**

SIZE:
**Male 80–97 cm long; female 74–85 cm**

SCIENTIFIC NAME:
**Menura novaehollandiae**

# Cock of the rock

FOUND IN:
**Northern South America**

SIZE:
**30 cm long**

SCIENTIFIC NAME:
***Rupicola rupicola***

FOUND IN:
**Eastern South America**

SIZE:
**20 cm long**

SCIENTIFIC NAME:
***Furnarius rufus***

The male cock of the rock is one of the most brilliantly coloured of all birds. In the breeding season, male birds perform spectacular group displays, competing for the attention of females. They leap into the air, flick their wings, and make noisy calls. Females have much plainer, mostly brown plumage. The cock of the rock lives in forests and feeds mainly on fruit.

Only the male superb lyrebird has the long, lyre-shaped tail. In the breeding season, he displays to the female, spreading his shimmering tail feathers over himself and dancing. The lyrebird rarely flies but hops and flaps up into trees to roost at night. It searches on the ground for insects to eat, scratching with its big, strong feet to uncover its prey.

# White-plumed antbird

FOUND IN:
**South America: Amazon basin**

SIZE:
**10 cm long**

SCIENTIFIC NAME:
***Pithys albifrons***

This antbird follows columns of army ants, which march through the forest. It eats other insects, which try to flee as the ants approach.

# FOCUS ON: *Birds of paradise*

Birds of paradise are named for their beautiful plumage and are among the most spectacular of all birds. While some are mainly black, with bright patches of shimmering iridescent feathers, others are coloured brilliant blue, red and yellow. Many have long, strangely shaped feathers on their head or tail.

There are more than 40 different species, ranging in size from about 13 to 107 centimetres long. Most live in the highland rainforests of New Guinea, but a few birds of paradise are found in the nearby Moluccan Islands and the forests of northeast Australia. Fruit is their main food, but they also catch insects, spiders and occasionally frogs and lizards.

Only the males have the colourful and decorative head and tail feathers for which the birds of paradise are famed. They use this ornate plumage in the courtship dances they perform to attract females. The female birds look quite different from the males, with dull, usually brownish plumage.

**King of Saxony bird**
*Wire-like plumes, up to 50 centimetres long, extend from the head of this bird. During courtship, these are held high.*

**An upside-down display**
*The blue bird of paradise hangs upside down in his efforts to attract females. His long tail streamers form a graceful arc over the cascade of magnificent blue plumage.*

**A group display**
*Most birds of paradise display alone, but the Raggianas gather in groups. When females appear, the males hop around, flapping their wings and calling. Each then tries to outdo the others in showing off his glorious plumage. At the peak of the display, the birds make a series of high-pitched calls.*

**Ribbon-tailed
bird of paradise**
*The male ribbon-tailed bird
has patches of shining green
feathers around his head and
long, ribbon-like tail feathers.
Nearly 1 metre long, these
tail feathers are twitched
from side to side as the bird
displays to females.*

**Tail plumes**
*Wilson's bird of paradise
has two coiled tail
feathers. These are held
at right angles to the
body when the
bird displays.*

**Lesser bird
of paradise**
*This bird shows off
its magnificent tail
plumes during its
courtship display.*

# Shore lark

Only the male bird has black tufts of feathers on his head. He raises them during courtship displays or when defending territory. Like other larks, this bird eats seeds, buds and insects.

FOUND IN:
**Europe, Asia and North America**

SIZE:
**15 cm long**

SCIENTIFIC NAME:
**Eremophila alpestris**

# Red-whiskered bulbul

FOUND IN:
**China, Nepal and India**

SIZE:
**20 cm long**

SCIENTIFIC NAME:
**Pycnonotus jocosus**

Flocks of these lively, noisy birds gather to feast on fruit trees, where they eat both ripe and unripe fruit.

# Northern parula

This little warbler eats insects, especially caterpillars, in trees. It creeps over the branches and hops from perch to perch as it looks for prey. It makes its nest in hanging tree lichen or Spanish moss. The female usually lays four or five eggs.

FOUND IN:
**North America**

SIZE:
**10 cm long**

SCIENTIFIC NAME:
**Parula americana**

The tiny northern wren has a plump body and a short tail, which it nearly always holds cocked up. Its main foods are insects and spiders, which it finds on low plants or in the undergrowth. In spring, the wren makes a nest of twigs, moss and grass in a hollow tree stump or among tree roots. The female lays five to eight eggs, which she incubates.

# Water pipit

The water pipit makes its nest in high mountain areas, usually close to rushing streams. In winter, harsh weather drives it down to damp lowland meadows.

FOUND IN:
**Europe and Asia**

SIZE:
**16 cm long**

SCIENTIFIC NAME:
**Anthus spinoletta**

# Northern wren

FOUND IN:
**North America, Europe, northern Africa and Asia**

SIZE:
**8–10 cm long**

SCIENTIFIC NAME:
**Troglodytes troglodytes**

# Great grey shrike

The great grey shrike is an aggressive bird with a strong, hooked beak. It keeps watch for prey from a high perch and makes short flights to catch insects. It also hunts by hovering in the air, waiting to pounce on small birds and mammals. Usually, the shrike carries its catch back to a perch to eat, but when food is plentiful this expert hunter catches extra prey and hangs it on a branch to store for another time.

FOUND IN:
**North America, Asia, Europe and northern Africa**

SIZE:
**23–25 cm long**

SCIENTIFIC NAME:
**Lanius excubitor**

# Northern mockingbird

FOUND IN:
**North America**

SIZE:
**23–28 cm long**

SCIENTIFIC NAME:
**Mimus polyglottos**

One of the best-known American songbirds, this mockingbird is the state bird of five U.S. states. The male sings night and day and often mimics other birds and sounds.

# Eastern bluebird

The eastern bluebird often perches on wires and fences but takes most of its insect prey on the ground. The male bluebird performs acrobatic flight displays to court his mate. Both birds then build a nest of grass and twigs in a tree hole or hollow stump.

FOUND IN:
**North and Central America**

SIZE:
**15–18 cm long**

SCIENTIFIC NAME:
**Sialia sialis**

# Willow warbler

The willow warbler catches insects in the air or picks them from leaves. In winter, when there are fewer insects in the north, it flies south to Africa.

FOUND IN:
**Europe, Africa and Asia**

SIZE:
**10 cm long**

SCIENTIFIC NAME:
**Phylloscopus trochilus**

# American robin

This bird lives everywhere from city suburbs to mountainsides. Earthworms are a favourite food, and the robin's sharp eyes help it spot worm burrows in the ground. It also eats snails and fruit.

FOUND IN:
**North America**

SIZE:
**23–28 cm long**

SCIENTIFIC NAME:
**Turdus migratorius**

# *B*lue flycatcher

With its blue plumage and fan of tail feathers, this is one of the most beautiful African flycatchers. Male and female look very similar, but young birds have paler blue feathers. This flycatcher is alert and always active. Insects are its main food. It watches from a perch, darting out to catch its prey in the air.

**FOUND IN:**
**Western Africa**

**SIZE:**
**13–15 cm long**

**SCIENTIFIC NAME:**
*Elminia longicauda*

# *E*uropean robin

**FOUND IN:**
**Europe, northern Africa and Asia**

**SIZE:**
**14 cm long**

**SCIENTIFIC NAME:**
*Erithacus rubecula*

The European robin is easily recognized by its orange-red breast and face. In many areas it is a shy forest bird, but in Britain and parts of Europe the robin lives in gardens and often becomes quite tame. Insects, spiders, worms and snails are the robin's main food, but it will also eat berries, small fruit and any scraps of food put out by humans. In the breeding season, the female robin makes a cup-shaped nest in a bush or hedge, or in a hole in a tree, wall or bank. She usually lays five or six eggs. Her mate helps her to feed and care for their young.

# FOCUS ON: *Crows*

Crows and other members of the crow family, such as rooks, ravens, magpies and jays, are noisy and aggressive but are thought by some people to be the most intelligent of all birds. They are extremely adaptable, eat almost anything, and often show their quick thinking in the clever ways they find to take new foods or steal from other birds.

There are more than a hundred different species of crow living all over the world, except in Antarctica and New Zealand. Most crows are large compared to other songbirds and have powerful, often hooked, beaks. Crows' legs are also strong, allowing them to move fast on the ground as well as in the air. While ravens, rooks and the crows are black, other members of the family such as jays and some magpies are brightly coloured.

### Rooks in flight
*Glossy black rooks breed in colonies at the top of tall trees, each pair making its own nest of sticks and twigs. A large rookery can be a noisy place as the birds squawk and caw in fights over space and nest material.*

### The cunning crow
*Of all birds, the crow has been one of the most successful at learning to live alongside humans. It scavenges for rubbish and visits gardens and farms in search of food.*

### Woodland bird
*The harsh screech of the jay is a familiar sound in woodlands, where this bird searches for insects and nuts. Acorns are among the jay's favourite foods, and it stores supplies for the winter months.*

### Magpie robbers

Magpies are well known for their thieving habits. They rob the nests of game birds, taking their eggs and young, and are also attracted to bright, shiny objects, such as bottle tops and even jewellery, which they take to their nests.

### The powerful raven

The raven is the largest of the crows and the biggest of all the songbird group. It is strong enough to kill and eat an animal as big as a rabbit, but it often feeds on carrion – the bodies of animals that are already dead.

### Jackdaw

The jackdaw nests in holes in trees and cliffs, but it has also learned to use spaces in chimneys and church towers. It eats almost anything from caterpillars to crabs, and robs the nests of other birds.

# $B$lack-capped chickadee

This little bird is easily identified by its call, which sounds like "chick-a-dee-dee-dee". Always on the move, it hops from branch to branch, searching for caterpillars and other insects as well as seeds and berries. It makes its nest in a hole it digs in the soft wood of a dead tree.

FOUND IN:
**North America**

SIZE:
**13 cm long**

SCIENTIFIC NAME:
*Parus atricapillus*

# $C$ardinal honeyeater

The cardinal honeyeater feeds by sipping nectar from flowers and picking insects from leaves. The female is duller than the vividly coloured male. She has olive grey feathers with red patches. This bird's cup-shaped nest hangs from a forked branch, and the female lays two or three eggs.

FOUND IN:
**Islands of Vanuatu, Samoa and Solomons**

SIZE:
**13 cm long**

SCIENTIFIC NAME:
*Myzomela cardinalis*

# $C$ardinal

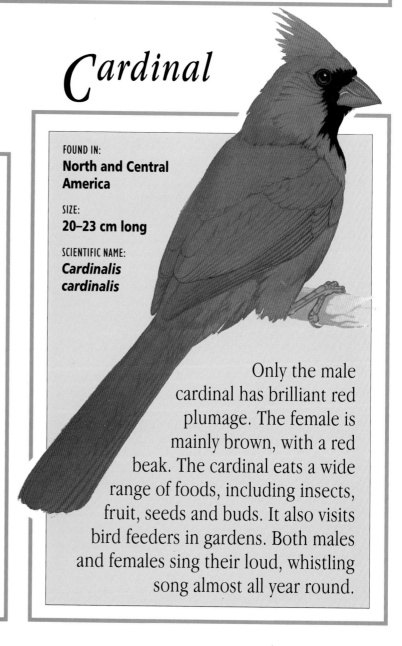

FOUND IN:
**North and Central America**

SIZE:
**20–23 cm long**

SCIENTIFIC NAME:
*Cardinalis cardinalis*

Only the male cardinal has brilliant red plumage. The female is mainly brown, with a red beak. The cardinal eats a wide range of foods, including insects, fruit, seeds and buds. It also visits bird feeders in gardens. Both males and females sing their loud, whistling song almost all year round.

# Yellow-backed sunbird

Female

Male

This sunbird eats flower nectar as well as insects. Sometimes it feeds like a hummingbird, hovering before tube-shaped flowers and reaching into them with its long tongue. But when feeding from large blooms such as hibiscus, it pierces the petals to reach the nectar at the base.

FOUND IN:
**India, Sumatra, Borneo and Malaysia**

SIZE:
**10 cm long**

SCIENTIFIC NAME:
*Aethopyga siparaja*

# Snow bunting

The snow bunting breeds further north than any other land bird and sometimes burrows in the snow to escape the cold. After breeding, it flies south for the winter. Seeds, insects and grasses are its main foods.

FOUND IN: **Arctic region**

SIZE: **16 cm long**

SCIENTIFIC NAME: *Plectrophenax nivalis*

# Scarlet tanager

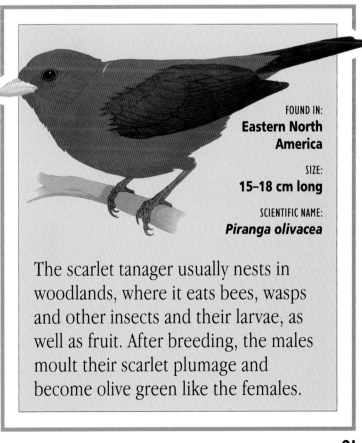

FOUND IN:
**Eastern North America**

SIZE:
**15–18 cm long**

SCIENTIFIC NAME:
*Piranga olivacea*

The scarlet tanager usually nests in woodlands, where it eats bees, wasps and other insects and their larvae, as well as fruit. After breeding, the males moult their scarlet plumage and become olive green like the females.

# Nightingale

Best known for its beautiful song, the nightingale sings both night and day. It eats insects such as ants and beetles, which it finds on the ground and in the undergrowth. In summer, it also eats berries and fruits.

FOUND IN:
**Europe, Asia and northern Africa**

SIZE:
**15 cm long**

SCIENTIFIC NAME:
***Luscinia megarhynchos***

# Northern oriole

FOUND IN:
**North, Central and South America**

SIZE:
**15–20 cm long**

SCIENTIFIC NAME:
***Icterus galbula***

The northern oriole lives in woodlands and searches trees and bushes for buds, fruit and insects to eat. A breeding pair makes a nest, which is woven from strands of plant material and has an opening at the top. After breeding, the birds migrate to Central and South America.

# Golden oriole

Although its plumage is so bright, the golden oriole is surprisingly well camouflaged in the light and shade of woodlands and forest. Most of its life is spent in the trees, feeding on insects and fruit with its sharp beak. It only rarely comes down to the ground. Its nest is like a tiny hammock made of grass and hangs from a forked branch.

# Blue jay

FOUND IN:
**North America**

SIZE:
**30 cm long**

SCIENTIFIC NAME:
***Cyanocitta cristata***

# House sparrow

FOUND IN:
**Europe, Asia
and northwest
Africa**

SIZE:
**25 cm long**

SCIENTIFIC NAME:
*Oriolus oriolus*

Female

Male

The house sparrow has been introduced worldwide and is an extremely adaptable bird. Seeds are its main food, but it also feeds on scraps put out by humans.

FOUND IN:
**Europe
and Asia**

SIZE:
**13–18 cm long**

SCIENTIFIC NAME:
*Passer domesticus*

# Starling

The starling lives both in country and city areas and eats many different foods. Starlings have been introduced into areas outside their natural range. Only a century ago, 60 birds were released in New York. Now, the starling is one of the most common birds in North America.

FOUND IN:
**Europe and western Asia;
introduced in
North America**

SIZE:
**20 cm long**

SCIENTIFIC NAME:
*Sturnus
vulgaris*

Noisy groups of blue jays are a familiar sight in gardens. Seeds and nuts are their main foods, and they bury extra supplies to save for the winter. Blue jays also eat insects and even steal eggs and chicks from the nests of other birds. A breeding pair makes its nest in a tree or bush, and the female lays two to six eggs. She usually incubates the eggs, but the male bird brings her food and helps to care for the young.

# Glossary

*You may find it useful to know the meanings of these words when reading this book.*

**Camouflage**
The colours or patterns on a bird's feathers that help it to hide in its surroundings so it cannot be seen by enemies or prey.

**Carrion**
The bodies of creatures that have died of natural causes or been killed by other animals. Vultures and condors are among the birds that feed on carrion.

**Colony**
A group of birds or other animals that live together. Gannets and penguins are some of the birds that live in colonies. The members of a colony are normally all of the same species, but mixed colonies do occur.

**Courtship display**
A series of movements designed to attract the attention of possible mates. Displays are usually performed by male birds, but in some species, such as great crested grebes, males and females display together. Courtship displays also help birds make sure that they are mating with the right species.

**Down feathers**
Soft feathers that lie underneath a bird's main feathers and help to keep the bird warm.

**Hovering**
A particular kind of flight in which the bird stays in one place in mid-air either to feed from a flower or to watch prey. Hummingbirds, for example, are expert hoverers, as are kestrels, which use their long tails to steady themselves.

**Incubation**
The process of keeping eggs warm until they hatch. Most birds do this by sitting on the eggs and warming them with the heat of their own body. The malleefowl, however, keeps its eggs warm by burying them in sand and rotting plants.

**Lek**
A specialized display performed by a group of male birds, such as grouse, to attract and impress females. Such displays take place in the same areas year after year. These areas are also sometimes called leks or lekking grounds.

**Migration**
The regular movement of a group of birds from one area to another. Migratory birds usually travel from areas where they breed in spring and summer to warmer areas nearer the equator where they spend the winter months.

**Nectar**
A sugary liquid produced by flowers to attract insects. Birds such as hummingbirds and sunbirds feed on nectar.

**Nest**
The place where a bird lays its eggs. Nests can range from simple scrapes on the ground to ornate woven structures in trees.

**Plumage**
The feathers covering a bird.

**Prey**
Creatures that are hunted and eaten by birds and other animals.

**Rainforest**
Forested areas near the equator, which are hotter and wetter than any other forests.

**Reptile**
A cold-blooded, scaly-skinned animal. Lizards, snakes, turtles and crocodiles are all reptiles.

**Roosting**
When birds are resting or sleeping, they are said to be roosting. The place where they rest is called a roost. Most birds roost at night, although night-feeders, such as owls, roost during the day.

**Species**
A particular type of bird. Members of the same species can mate and produce young, which in turn can have young themselves. Birds of different species cannot do this.

**Territory**
The area where a bird normally lives and feeds. Some birds defend their territory fiercely.

**Tundra**
A cold region in the far north of the earth where there are no tall trees, only low-growing plants. North America, northern Europe and Asia have tundra regions.

# Index

# Acknowledgements

### ILLUSTRATION CREDITS

Description of birds on pages 14–15, 18–21, 26–27, 30–31, 36–37, 40–41, 46–47, 54–55, 58–59, 64–65, 68–71, 74–75, 80–81, 84–87, 90–93 by:
Norman Arlott, Hilary Burn, Chris Christoforou, Robert Gillmor, Peter Hayman, Denys Ovenden, David Quinn, Andrew Robinson, Chris Rose, David Thelwell,
Owen Williams, Ken Wood, Michael Woods

Pages 8–9 by Peter D. Scott/Wildlife Art Agency

Pages 16–17, 28–29, 38–39, 48–49, 56–57, 66–67, 72–73, 82–83, 88–89 by Michael Woods

Pages 12–13, 24–25, 34–35, 44–45, 52–53, 62–63, 78–79 by Bruce Pearson/Wildlife Art Agency

### PHOTOGRAPHIC CREDITS

9 Richard Packwood/Oxford Scientific Films;  10–11 Nicholas Devore/Bruce Coleman;  17 Mark Hamblin/Oxford Scientific Films;
22–23 Ben Osborne/Oxford Scientific Films;  28 Colin Monteath/Oxford Scientific Films;  32–33 David Cayless/Oxford Scientific Films;
39 Frank Schneidermeyer/Oxford Scientific Films;  42–43 Belinda Wright/Oxford Scientific Films;  49 Mike McKavett/Bruce Coleman;  50–51 Breck P. Kent/Animals
Animals/Oxford Scientific Films;  57 Wendy Shattil and Bob Rozinski/Oxford Scientific Films;  60–61 Zefa Picture Library;  66 Steve Turner/Oxford Scientific Films;
72 Michael Fogden/Oxford Scientific Films;  76–77 Wayne Lankinen/Bruce Coleman;  83 J.R. MacKinnon/Bruce Coleman;  88 Barry Walker/Oxford Scientific Films